From the Closet to the Courts

From the Closet to the Courts

The Lesbian Transition

Ruth Simpson

A Richard Seaver Book
The Viking Press
New York

This book is dedicated to each and every lesbian.
By living with personal and political integrity,
we may, one day, live in complete freedom.

Copyright © 1976 by Ruth Simpson
All rights reserved
A Richard Seaver Book/The Viking Press
First published in 1976 by The Viking Press, Inc.
625 Madison Avenue, New York, N.Y. 10022
Published simultaneously in Canada by
The Macmillan Company of Canada Limited
Printed in U.S.A.

Library of Congress Cataloging in Publication Data
Simpson, Ruth, 1926–
    From the closet to the courts.
    "A Richard Seaver book."
    1. Lesbianism.   2. Homosexuality.   I.   Title.
HQ76.S54   301.41'57   75–25658
ISBN 0–670–33165–1

ACKNOWLEDGMENTS: Journal of the American Medical Association: from
Homosexuality and Medicine by Dr. Charles W. Socarides (May 18, 1970,
pp. 1199–1202), Copyright © 1970, American Medical Association. Little,
Brown and Company and the Sterling Lord Agency: from *The Love That
Dared Not Speak Its Name* by H. Montgomery Hyde, Copyright © 1970 by
Harford Productions, Ltd. Reprinted by permission.

Contents

Introduction

Some writers have regrets about their books. I regret that my parents were never able to read this work. My father died at the age of forty-eight in 1947; my mother died in 1962—she was sixty-two. They had known each other since my mother was five and my father six. They went through grade school and high school together. My father went to France during World War I, while my mother taught school. When he returned they were married. They loved each other well and long. They loved my two older brothers and me with great care and imagination.

From open hands they gave me values which I treasure and which have been re-enforced by my own experiences. Having been pioneers in the early days of the labor movement, they were two of the first few who fought for the civil rights of all people in that movement. Their concern for each other, for me, and for people in general was based on respect for human dignity. Despite the poverty in which we lived for many years, I had a gentle and lovely childhood.

If, indeed, the parental model is instrumental in shaping the child's future life, I should be heterosexual. All the joy I experienced as a child from my parents' happy marriage, however, has done nothing to alter the fact that I am a lesbian.

As early as I can remember, I knew that I preferred girls. I never thought that there was anything unusual about this until I was in my teens. At that point—since it was what young women were conditioned to do—I had a relationship with a young man. I even considered marrying him. Fortunately for him, for me, and for any child we might have had, I did not.

Subsequently I had my first serious lesbian relationship. Like many first loves, that one, though still remembered, was soon over—after a year and a half of joy and pain.

As an English/Drama major in college, I became active in both university and community theater in Cleveland, Ohio, where I was born and grew up. After my father's death, before I was twenty-one, I left for New York to become involved in the theater; I had, however, formed the habits of eating regularly, paying rent, and staying reasonably clothed. The "maybe next year" evasions expressed by theater people in what has always been a glutted field caused me to leave my "career" after one off-off Broadway play and two years of making the rounds of interviews and readings.

By sheer chance I got a job in a public relations firm, and a few years later found that I had become a public relations executive. I pursued this career until 1969 when I became involved in the homosexual movement.

During those years in the business world I was closeted. The long and serious relationship I had with one woman had to be kept secret from practically all of our mutual heterosexual friends.

Though my mother visited us and obviously understood our relationship, we never discussed it. When I would visit her in Ohio and friends there would ask the inevitable question, "Well, Ruth, when are you going to get married?" as often as not my mother would answer with something like, "She hasn't met a man she wants to marry. She is doing very well for herself, and I am proud of her."

During all those years I buried my concern for those working in movements, despite some peripheral involvement in some causes. During 1956, for example, I worked on membership drives for the N.A.A.C.P. and, later, went on occasional civil rights marches or demonstrations. This social apathy (days would go by without my reading the news) was a direct result of my reaction to my parents' experiences in a labor movement that did not treat them kindly. Fragmentation, diversion of goals, infiltrators, and foot-dragging people unwilling to support the movement's real goals all conspired to bring my parents and the movement to grief time after time. I wanted no part of the deceptions and confusion of such a life.

I had been living alone for more than twelve years, having rare and transient lesbian relationships when, in 1969, I went to my first meeting of Daughters of Bilitis, New York, a lesbian organization. There I saw women who carried psychic scars. I remember thinking, "I have come home to my people. Perhaps all of us working together can start to change things so the young ones coming up will not have to suffer in the same way."

D.O.B., New York, was one of the chapters of the National D.O.B. formed in San Francisco in 1955. Its ambiance was socio-educational, but from 1969 through early 1971 it became active in the political sense and gained visibility via the mass media. As soon as it reached viability it began to disintegrate for a combination of reasons: police harassment, agent infiltration, internal disruption, and the apathy of its membership about reacting with purpose against these fragmenting elements. During this period, in addition to work in the homosexual movement, I worked in conjunction with those in other movements—blacks, Hispanics, poor, and feminists. I learned that most movement organizations which achieve political visibility suffer from the same ills, and that many doers have been turned aside by the disrupters. Today D.O.B., New York, is gone, along with some others of its contemporary groups.

I learned—this time not vicariously through my parents —that movement work is pretty much the same, no matter what the issue. I am wiser for the hard lessons the movement taught me; and I am grateful for the fact that through it I met Ellen Povill. We have lived together for only about four years, but these years have been constant proof that lesbianism can offer the beauty and equality of love which my mother and father found in their heterosexuality. That is why I am sorry they did not read my book—they would have liked it.

All oppressed people have a lot to learn from one another, since closets are the cocoons of all minority movements. These closets are deceptively comforting—until their seemingly safe space becomes too restrictive for the spirit. Anyone who breaks the confines of the cocoon is soon radicalized by our culture's response. When this happens, the result is usually a short, painful trip from the closet to the courts.

Homosexuals are a giant step behind other oppressed groups. We are labeled by the laws in most states as extralegal. Our first step, and it is indeed a giant one, is to remove ourselves from criminal status by removing archaic federal and state sex laws from the books. It may quickly be said, "You can't legislate attitudes." That is true, but nonetheless we must work toward placing ourselves on legally acceptable ground.

The various cocoons which house the closeted masses of minority members are separate and different from one another. Each group fears the emerging butterfly from the alien cocoon. Homosexuals crosscut all sectors of society: we come in all colors, nationalities, religions, in both sexes, and from every economic and educational background. Our multiple heritage is our strength, though to date it has not been utilized.

As the pattern of oppressive action toward all minority groups is the same, we all must try to understand the similarity of our causes, at the same time realizing and respecting the nature of our differences. Through this understanding a coalition could arise: we would become a patchwork majority, a dangerous potential for any oppressor.

As a homosexual I am obligated to my own people; as a woman I am responsible to feminist principles; as a human being I am dedicated to the basic right of human dignity. Each of these responsibilities will be met to the best of my ability as I deal with the specific problems of the lesbian as particularly illustrative of problems which confront every member of any oppressed group who takes a step away from the hiding place toward that hostile ground known as our society.

From the Closet to the Courts

1
What Is Lesbianism?
Myths and Facts

The first myth about lesbianism to be dealt with is the "clinically accepted definition" of a lesbian. This definition was developed by a panel of male psychiatrists: "A lesbian is an adult female who is engaging in overt, repetitive homosexual activity." It is immediately clear that the definition is circular, and it certainly begs the question. It is as illuminating as defining a pear tree, to a person who has no concept of trees or pears, by saying that a pear tree is a tree that grows pears. If we adapt the statement of the psychiatric panel and apply it to the heterosexual woman—"any adult female who is engaging in repetitive overt heterosexual activity"—it becomes glaringly apparent that many heterosexual women would be excluded from their heterosexual class.

The word "lesbian" can characterize many various conditions which are neither mutually exclusive nor necessarily mutually inclusive in any particular case: being a woman who is involved in a love relationship with another woman; being a woman who spends more time with women than with men; being a woman who has sexual relations with another woman; being a woman who loves women; being a woman who prefers being with women to being with men; being a woman who has sexual relations with men but prefers a love relationship with a woman; being a woman who does not have sexual relations with men, and so on.

The alleged necessary and sufficient criterion for being a lesbian as stated in the psychiatrists' definition raises many questions: What of the woman who has had no heterosexual activity and has had one homosexual relationship? Is she to be considered a non-lesbian? What of the woman who has experienced covert feelings of sexual and/or emotional attraction to other women but has engaged in no homosexual activity? Is she to be considered a heterosexual? And what of the virgin? If a heterosexual woman without any sexual experience is considered a virgin, it may be assumed that a woman who loves another woman but has had no homosexual activity should be referred to as a lesbian virgin. But the necessary and sufficient condition for lesbianism as stated by the panel places such a woman in some sort of limbo; obviously she cannot be categorized as a lesbian. What of the woman who has had a long lesbian relationship which might have ended years ago and who is currently sexually dormant? Is she to be considered heterosexual, or does she also fall in the category of non-definition? Is she also excluded from her class?

It all becomes a maze that is so labyrinthine, repetitive, and exclusively sexual in orientation as to become ridiculous; and we soon realize that the myth of the clinically accepted definition of a lesbian is used not so much to en-

4

lighten and describe as to limit and distort. It uses two words which threaten the security of the non-homosexual psyche— lesbian and homosexual—to alienate, by mystification, the non-homosexual from the homosexual.

Heterosexuality, it should be noted, has not been given any such a "clinically accepted definition" based on psychiatric "research" of disturbed heterosexual women who needed psychiatric help. It is not, in fact, the way to develop a medical description of any sort of sexual persuasion. One must consider the many lesbians who have—despite our restrictive, oppressive, and sexist society—adjusted happily to lesbianism. And what of the lesbians who go to psychiatrists not because of their lesbianism, but because of the myriad pressures imposed on the individual by our culture? What of the lesbians who have emotional problems because they come from broken heterosexual marriages? What of the lesbians who were molested by heterosexual males when they were children? What of the lesbians who can't see what is wrong with loving a woman per se, but who have been influenced all their lives to believe, because of religious, social, and family pressures, that there is something basically "wrong" with a woman who doesn't become a wife and mother?

From these questions it may be deduced that there is a double standard in both the understanding of and the "accepted" attitudes toward lesbianism.

Most people believe, if they have ever given it any thought, that they already know what heterosexuality is. They also are sure they know what lesbianism is because it has been defined for them by the government, the church, and the medical professions. The fact is, it has been defined by people who have no actual concept of lesbianism and/or by people who, through enlightened self-interest, prefer to keep the lesbian separate from the rest of her class—women —and homosexuals in general separate from other oppressed groups.

Sociologists use the word "myth" to mean a collective belief that is built up in response to the wishes of the group rather than to an analysis of the basis of the wishes. The *bases* of the wishes of our institutions are all reflected in the myth-wishes of society in general:

1. *Lesbians are man-haters.* Lesbianism is not so negative a thing. It is based on positive emotion: a woman loves/ likes women. Usually, lesbians do not regard men in any specific sexual-emotional way and have in some instances developed freer relationships with men than many heterosexual women have been able to form. They are not bound by the challenge-competition syndrome which keeps heterosexual women in the position of climbing from the bottom of the ladder, against many odds, in the most "lady-like" way possible in order to conceal the fact that someone is stepping on their fingers as they reach each rung. Our society regards any woman who functions independently of men as a threat to the system, i.e., the male status, the family, procreation. If she functions well, lives a whole emotional, physical, intellectual life, the woman is a "misfit." She has broken out of her cocoon of false security in a society which is built on the male-female role system. Therefore, she must hate men, by and for whom the system was built and is sustained. That she can relate to men in a mutual exchange of humanity is not considered possible. Every woman should have the option of enjoying whatever exchange of compassion, dignity, and beauty pleases her. It is often said that a true friendship cannot exist between a man and a woman. Who hates men? The thought of loving another human being with whom there is no possibility

6

of friendship implies a rejection of human dignity. This is as close to hating as anyone should wish to come.

2. *Women are lesbians because they can't get a man.* This myth-wish relegates lesbianism to a negative result rather than a positive choice. Any self-determining action on the part of a woman is threatening to the male-dominated society. The active choice of a woman as a love partner by a woman is a quintessential threat.

This notion of the lesbian as an unsuccessful woman, one unable to "get a man," is often expressed by heterosexual women. To such a woman, who has accepted her second-class status and male-supporting role, lesbianism throws into question her own negation of self-value. For her it is difficult to acknowledge that a woman could love another woman, for she does not consider woman (herself) worthy.

Something so alien as lesbianism is to our society must be explained away and dealt with by a class myth. This is much simpler than facing the basis for the wish itself: oppression of women.

3. *Women become lesbians because they are afraid of childbirth or don't like children.* As of 1971, approximately one third of the members of Daughters of Bilitis were mothers. Many women who have children and who love their children very much have either suppressed their lesbianism while married or developed a lesbian relationship subsequent to the dissolution of their marriages. A number of lesbian couples have raised or are rearing children quite happily. Many lesbian partners would like very much to adopt and give good homes to children who need homes so desperately. However, since avowed lesbians are extra-legal, or, as the law books put it, "of bad moral character," they are not permitted to adopt. It is, simply, unsubstantiated that the percentage of lesbian women who

7

fear childbirth is larger or more definitive than that of heterosexual women.

4. *All lesbians are really in love with their fathers.* This
myth-wish obviates the need to accept the fact that one
woman can love and be happy with another woman by pur-
porting that she can and really does love a man: her father.
But many lesbians have expressed feelings of dislike for
oppressive fathers. In some instances, the fathers have
beaten the mothers and the children. This understandably
does not make an attractive love object for any woman who
refuses to accept brutalization as a way of life. Many lesbians, however, love and like one or both of their parents
very much. In other words, lesbians who obviously have
come from heterosexual households have the same responses
to the happinesses or traumas of these individual households as do heterosexuals. There is no extra wrinkle in the
lesbian brain which makes her react differently from the
non-lesbian to her early family environment.

5. *Women become lesbians because they had a bad experience with men in their early lives.* Just ask around. Most
women, both lesbian and heterosexual, have had a "bad"
experience at one time or another—unless they are extremely fortunate. The societal myth-wish of the "bad experience" seems to connote that if only the right man had
got to her in time, she might not have ended up a lesbian.
Again, the other side of the coin: Are women heterosexual
because they had a "bad experience" with men in their early
lives? If the right woman had got to her in time, she might
not have ended as a heterosexual. Our male-oriented society
does not *need* this myth. Heterosexuality *needs* no *raison
d'être.*

The reasons given for lesbianism in psychiatric case studies are many: an oppressive father, an aggressive mother,

8

being an only child, sibling rivalry, and so on ad infinitum. In fact, so many reasons are given for lesbianism that one might well wonder how anybody achieves heterosexuality.

6. *Feminists are really lesbians.* The epithet "lesbian" (carrying with it all its mythical ramifications) is hurled at the feminist in an attempt to undermine her credibility as a woman and to intimidate her back into her "place." Not only are many heterosexual feminists still frightened by lesbianism and victimized by the abounding misinformation about it, some lesbians still function within oppressive relationships, having transferred role patterns from heterosexual models. The former are not lesbians; the latter are not feminists.

7. *All lesbians are either "butch" or "femme."* Some lesbians are one or the other. Many, however, are not, since they feel that adoption of oppressive roles is too binding for an entirely free relationship. Many of us feel extremely proud of our love for women and assume that neither woman in a lesbian relationship wants or needs anything other than a woman for emotional, sexual, and intellectual fulfillment, the feeling being: if I wanted a man, it would be easy enough to have one; but, very simply, I am happier with a woman.

Those lesbians who are in butch-femme relationships are in some instances very happy, and the entire purpose of the homosexual movement is to establish the freedom to love the person of one's choice and to be loved by the person of one's choice in whatever way best sustains both partners' sense of dignity, beauty, and equilibrium. That there should be restrictions on such freedom is a dread comment on humanity.

The butch-femme myth-wish evolved no doubt from the fact that what is referred to as the "obvious" lesbian is indeed what is seen and "recognized" by society in general. It is also probably a breeding ground for "confirmation" of some of the other myths surrounding lesbianism. Since it is only "obvious" lesbians whom society sees, it is a natural next step to think, "It's clear that they want a man-woman relationship, since that is what they are acting out, but they can't form one because they: (must hate men) (are afraid of childbirth) (were unable to get a man) (are in love with their fathers) . . ." and all of the other previously stated myth-wishes.

Those lesbians who adopt butch-femme roles should have the same option and acceptance accorded the heterosexual woman who is into the "I don't expect my man to do anything that isn't masculine" female role. The two actually function in the same sexual-emotional ambiance.

To clarify another aspect of lesbianism: if twenty lesbians were asked to define homosexuality they would probably give twenty different personal definitions. The same would no doubt be true of twenty heterosexual women asked to define heterosexuality. It is almost certain that not one of the heterosexual women would say that heterosexuality is a disinclination to love a woman.

Lesbianism is not a disinclination to love men; it is, rather, an inclination, a positive, empathic, emotional, and, in most instances, physical response to another woman. But lesbianism is by no means an exclusively sexual term. It implies involvement on all levels of consciousness.

In self-protection from the attitudes arising from and described in the myth-wishes of society, many women repress their lesbian orientation. Some are wives and mothers; others never marry and may never have a sexual relationship with another woman but spend most of their lives with other women. Some may do so comfortably; many others, however, lead lives of frustration, not because they don't have men but rather because they don't have *women*. The woman who is referred to derogatorily as "a frustrated old maid" is not necessarily frustrated because she is without a man. If she is frustrated she may be so because our society has placed her in the position of thinking that loving another woman is "immoral," therefore unavailable to her as a way of life. She is denied emotional and physical sustenance because of fears and anxieties which our culture has built up around lesbianism.

There is another group of women, a step removed from the one just described, who know they are lesbians, who often form lesbian relationships, and who lead double lives, hoping that "people won't know." They often date men so that people won't wonder. They may play the game well and never express resentment of their forced double image. But to understand the psychological effect, imagine a heterosexual woman having to go through life pretending that she really doesn't like men very much and at the same time having to make a show of loving women. This kind of unnatural situation obviously should not be forced on anyone. No one should be fearful or guilt-ridden because she loves *anybody*. Society seems to forget that it is not love but hate that is immoral.

A general fact about lesbianism: there are more of us than most people realize, whether we are in or out of the closet, visible or invisible, whether we live whole, half, or double lives. There have been estimates of a homosexual population in this country of twenty million. It is impossible to give a truly accurate estimate, since so many homosexuals live totally closeted lives, and their numbers are not included in clinical, psychiatric, or organizational statistics. Those of us who work in the homosexual community are

11

assured that there are perhaps two or three unknown and uncounted homosexuals for each one who is counted.

The distribution of male and female homosexuals is approximately half and half. There may be more closeted female homosexuals than males, since women have a more difficult time making their way financially through life than men do and are, therefore, forced into more cautious, fearful deceptions.

Considering the homosexual's extra-legal status and the disregard in which we are held, what is perhaps most amazing is that so many of us have left the closet. Those of us who have must pull the weight for those who are still hidden. Each minority movement has to face this self-defeating problem. Not only is it lonely out there away from the closet, but some of those still closet-bound have self-deceptive and hurtful things to say, such as, "Don't stir up problems for me," the translation of which is, "If I get out of the closet somebody may expect me to *do* something, and I'm not ready for the responsibility." Or they may say: "I don't think I'm oppressed. What's all the fuss about?" Translation: "Don't rock the boat. I'm making it and it doesn't bother me that I have to live a lie." Or: "Why do you have to flaunt it?" Which may be interpreted as, "I'm afraid people will find out about me. I'm ashamed."

Lesbian identity, for example, has been slower in its development than black pride, because it is easier for homosexuals to hide in order to protect themselves against the myths. Women who are lesbians have no distinguishing lesbian color, dialect, or name. It is much easier to retreat from the responsibility of acknowledging that you are being denied your right to human dignity when you believe that "nobody needs to know" what you are doing. Too often it is true: "Nobody needs to know."

12

All minority members are the victims of myths about their particular minority. The myths about homosexuals should be questioned by all, just as myths about all other minorities should be questioned by us. For instance, I have heard "proud gays" speak disparagingly about the "bums on welfare," never questioning the validity of their "opinion," which is in actuality a myth. These people found somebody that they could denigrate to enhance their own feeling of "superiority."

We owe it to our individual intellects and to our collective sense of justice to avoid using myths that seem to make more attractive our own chancy status in a system which one way or another exploits all of us. Until we do, we will all have difficulty in establishing our own identities within the framework of a potentially just society. We have already learned that facile and misleading myths distort our own and others' identities, rendering social justice an impossibility.

2

The Family
There's No Hiding Place
Except the Closet

"Where Did We Go Wrong?"
—Headline for a series of articles on "Homosexuals in
New York," New York Post, *March 26, 1974.*

Usually the family is a safe haven for a minority-group child. Most often it offers the child security, insulation, and instruction against prejudice, bigotry, and hatred. The parent is the first person to whom the child turns for comfort and explanation . . . unless the child is homosexual.

The parent is unavailable to the homosexual child because (1) the stigma imposed on homosexuality by religious, educational, governmental, and medical institutions made it initially impossible for parents to understand homosexuality and (2) the child has already developed such a sense of shame about sexuality in general, such confusion, shame, and guilt about homosexuality specifically that communication between the uninformed child and the ill-advised parent is impossible. Many young homosexuals are disturbed not by their sexuality but by the anxiety caused by its being unexplained and unaccepted.

14

It is at this point that the lesbian's first hiding place starts building: the family closet. In many cases she never leaves its confines, leading a life of anxiety, loneliness, and corrupted self-image. Other minorities have closets, but they are not in the home and were not developed as a barrier between child and parent.

Homosexuals are increasingly outraged by the educational conditioning of both child and parent to fear and, in many instances, feel disgust toward the homosexual. Because of the long history of this conditioning, it is rare that a parent understands or accepts the homosexual child. Even if the parent is enlightened enough to "accept" the homosexuality of her daughter, she is still under constant tension because her friends might "find out." In any case, it is being damned by faint praise to be "accepted" by a parent, the one person who is "supposed to love us no matter what."

When a number of heterosexual women were asked how they would feel, and what they would do, should they learn that their daughters were lesbian, their responses were negative: "I would take her to a psychiatrist immediately and have her cured"; "I would rather she would get pregnant—at least that would be normal"; "I would see to it that she was married as soon as possible"; and a classic: "If her father ever found out he'd kill me." Small wonder that homosexuals, by the time they reach maturity, are so used to hiding that it often becomes a way of life.

Many parents feel they have "failed" when they learn their child is homosexual. They wonder what they "did that was wrong." This guilt is of course transferred to the lesbian, who in turn feels guilty for hurting her parents.

As president of D.O.B., New York, I received many letters from women all over the country (we averaged more than a hundred a week). Following is a fair example:

> Dear Miss Simpson,
> I doubt very much that this letter will be read but at least I feel better for writing it. I am a lesbian—and that is the first time I have ever put it down in writing. I have grown up in a very middle class atmosphere and therefore—what is taboo is *definitely* taboo. As a result, I am 23 yrs. old, unsuspected and unhappy.
> Well, I never realized there were organizations like D.O.B. until I read the article on this in the New York Time Magazine, so I guess I just want to say that it is comforting to know you're not alone and that some people care enough to start such an organization.
> I'm quite sure that I'll never be part of this organization because of the fears of being found out; *hurting others* [author's italics], etc. but if ever the world changes, it's at least nice to know that someone cared enough to have it there. Thank you.

Both child and parent are victims of the archaic attitudes about sexuality perpetuated by our culture.

*The New York Time*s of February 10, 1971, published an article by Jane E. Brody, "Homosexuality: Parents Aren't Always to Blame." The title alone clearly implies that *some*body or *some*thing is "to blame" for homosexuality. This is a terrible burden for the homosexual as well as for any person who wants to understand homosexuality and is trying to establish an intelligent attitude toward it.

The family closet, the only temporarily safe place for the young homosexual, cannot help alienating the child from the parent. As the young lesbian reaches her teens, she sometimes feels obligated to have sexual relations with a boy. Often, in such cases, she is motivated partly by the hope that her parents won't suspect her true sexuality. This adds fur-

16

ther to the sense of alienation and resentment that inevitably builds up between child and parent.

A number of lesbians have indicated how deeply distressed they were, after making the decision to be honest, to have to tell family members. Often the young woman's sexuality had already been guessed, and family responses ranged from "I wondered when you were going to figure it out" to "I knew you were different, but I couldn't really believe that someone in our family could be one of *those.*"

Such responses indicate the reluctance of most parents to explore and discuss the concept of homosexuality, despite the risk of damaging a family relationship and the psyche of a child. That non-understanding and fear of homosexuality have been perpetuated to such an extent is indeed some gauge of the unrealistic stress our society places on the "normal." Many parents prefer to ignore the subject, at the possible cost of total alienation and future psycho-emotional disturbance of the child, rather than to confront the "dread subject" of "deviate sexual behavior." It should be observed here that in many cases what our law books term "deviate sexual behavior" and label as a crime—which covers just about everything except the so-called missionary position—is in actuality practiced by the parents of homosexuals. The law, however, has practically never been pursued against heterosexuals.

In a number of instances, mothers of lesbians registered anxiety about their daughters' homosexuality on the basis that it reflected negatively on their own "femininity." These mothers felt that their daughters "couldn't get a man." It has never been said by any homosexual with whom I have talked nor have I read anything to date which suggests that the male homosexual is homosexual because he "can't get a woman." This appraisal is practically unheard of; the male *opts* for his sexuality, but the female is homosexual because for one reason or another she is unable to relate to a man.

Many women in today's society have clearly accepted the role they are expected to play. Take, for example, the article by Enid Nemy in the June 4, 1972, edition of *The New York Times* entitled "For These Women Marriage Is Enough." The piece included quotes from the wives of some of the country's leading business executives. Said Mrs. John E. Swearingen, "My husband likes to see me neat, well groomed and never fussy. . . . He expects me to be what I am . . . useful, punctual, efficient, pleasant, alert and healthy. He has no patience with the opposites of any of these. He wants me to be feminine, to have a sense of humor without being witty and not be too emphatic. I have learned quickly to compromise." Mrs. Graham J. Morgan expressed the belief that ". . . you don't pursue your own personal life . . . you gear yourself to your husband's life." Mrs. Lee Allen Muench finds happiness because "My husband's life has made me change my life completely on many occasions. . . . Oh, I'm taken for granted like most wives. But once in a while he says and does something that makes me feel important."

Imagine the dilemma of such women—and there are many, many of them—if they should find out that their daughters were lesbian. She, the mother, would be humiliated and stigmatized because her daughter refused to conform to the "normal" and love a man.

Despite the fact that women are defined and confined sociologically, emotionally, intellectually, and certainly financially by their sexuality; despite the marriage laws, statistics on women's employment, and all the other tangible manifestations of oppression of women which feminists have explored, iterated, and reiterated, many heterosexual women still proclaim that women are not oppressed in this patriarchal society. When such women find that a child of theirs is homosexual, they almost always react by asking that fateful question: What did I do wrong? They find it impossible to adjust to the notion of a lesbian daughter, to even consider the possibility that homosexuality is a natural phenomenon which has occurred all through history. Too often these women have heard from the medical profession that homosexuality is a sickness, from the church that it is a sin, from the business world that homosexuals are unemployable, from educators that homosexuality is a maladjustment, and from the law that homosexuality is a crime. The idea that homosexuality might be a valid alternate life style never occurs to them. Having heard that lesbianism is "caused by various combinations of familial relationships," they naturally experience paroxysms of guilt and self-recrimination. It never occurs to these mothers that despite all the heterosexual orientation female children receive from all sides, despite all the anti-homosexual propaganda female children receive from all sides, and despite all of the anxieties and fears a young girl might have about her homosexuality, she will still persist in her sexuality because it is to her a natural, positive persuasion which needs no statement of "definition" or "cause." It is, despite the frequent put-downs she hears and reads, as natural to her as heterosexuality is to her fear- and guilt-stricken parents.

In September 1971 I was invited, along with others either active in the homosexual movement or involved in related research, to testify at hearings at the New York Bar Association by the Assembly of New York State. The purpose of the testimony was to consider the intent and effect of existing laws concerning crimes without victims. At this series of hearings, Dr. Edward Pomeroy, a leading Kinsey researcher, testified in part that if laws against deviate sexual behavior were applied equally against all persons, ninety-five per cent of all males and eighty-five per cent of all females would be in jail. He also discussed the now-well-known Kinsey "0–to–6 Scale," zero on the scale representing those who are exclusively heterosexual, and six, those exclusively homosexual. The research done concerned itself exclusively with males. Of all males studied, eighteen per cent were three or higher on the scale.

Dr. Pomeroy pointed out that neither religion nor education was a factor, that sexual persuasion was not influenced in any sense of the word by ethnic or economic background. Dr. Pomeroy also talked of "animal behavior studies which have confirmed that homosexuality is a definite part of the mammalian culture." He said, "As a matter of fact, I once met a charming porcupine—he was a six, definitely a six."

The fears of homosexuality that so many parents have would be measurably decreased if accurate information were made available. The psyche-damaging anxieties experienced by countless lesbians who have no place to turn for information would be dissolved if unbiased studies were made of women homosexuals—unbiased in the sense that outmoded moral values and myth-wishes were not invoked against women—lesbian women specifically and all women in general.

During my six years in the forefront of the homosexual movement, I have talked with many hundreds of lesbians and, in a number of instances, with one or both parents; I have consulted with segments of other movements about some of

the problems they have in thinking of the homosexual movement as a political force rather than "a sort of fad thing,"
as some people have labeled it; I have lectured at Cornell
Medical School, New York University Medical, Saint Vincent's School of Nursing, and at many other schools and
colleges; I have participated in seminars on human sexuality, homosexuality, victimless crimes—endless discussions
which ultimately exposed the blatant misinformation that
is abroad and the attendant fears this misinformation
breeds. The primary recipient of this misinformation is the
family.

To cite a specific example: I receive numerous telephone
calls from women—lesbians and mothers of lesbians—with
questions. One conversation went like this:

CALLER: Is this the right Ruth Simpson? I was given your
name.

RUTH: Are you calling the Ruth Simpson from D.O.B.?
If so, I am the right person. Where did you get my name?

CALLER: Somebody gave it to me—well, at a gay bar. I
can't talk too loud because I'm calling from home and I
don't want anybody to hear me.

RUTH: How old are you—are you of age?

CALLER: Yes, I'm nineteen. But I just called because, well,
I've heard such terrible things and I think I am a lesbian.

RUTH: What terrible things have you been hearing—terrible things about what?

CALLER: Well, is there any place I can go to talk to someone about . . . where can I meet somebody like myself? I
am so upset.

RUTH: The Gay Activists Alliance has meetings for women
every Sunday afternoon.

CALLER: Yes, I know. I just called and it is closed.

RUTH: Look, I don't know how you feel about telling me your name, but what should I call you?

CALLER: (long pause) Well, you can call me "Alicia." Oh, I am so upset, and I hope I'm not bothering you.

RUTH: Fine, Alicia. No, of course you aren't bothering me. I am sorry you are upset. Can you tell me what particular thing is upsetting you? (long pause) Alicia, I share my life with Ellen Povill. She is past-vice-president of D.O.B. We have both talked to many young women who have been upset, just as you are, and sometimes we have been able to help them understand some of the problems involved. If you would like to meet with us, and if you have a friend whom you would like to bring along, you can.

ALICIA: Do you really mean that? Would it be a friendly atmosphere?

RUTH: Of course it will be a friendly atmosphere. What do you mean?

ALICIA: Well, that's what I mean. My mother told me that people like you get young women and make them lick up the floor or attack them.

RUTH: That is absolutely ridiculous. Where on earth did your mother get such an idea?

ALICIA: She just asks anybody in the neighborhood, like the man at the corner candy store, what they know about lesbians, and they tell her all this junk.

RUTH: You say it's junk, and it certainly is malicious and untrue, so you will have to think for yourself. Your mother obviously has fears which come from ignorance about homosexuality.

ALICIA: Well, you don't have a pseudo-male voice, or you don't sound like a Sister George type at all. My parents are just driving me crazy. They try to make me make dates all the time, and the pressure, and they tell me such horrible things. I've just got to get out of the house.

RUTH: Why don't you go out for a walk so you can be alone and think about things—there is nothing wrong about a woman having feelings of love for another woman. Why don't you think things over, and if you decide you would like to meet with us to talk things over, just give us a call.

I gave her my address and told her that my phone was tapped. (It has been for over five years.) At this point I explained that there is pressure put on all homosexuals and that this pressure is external, having nothing to do with homosexuality per se, adding that lesbianism is a natural and in many cases a beautiful thing.

Alicia thanked me and said that she would call back.

The following evening my telephone rang.

CALLER: Is this Mrs. Simpson?

RUTH: This is Miss Simpson.

CALLER: Oh, Miss Simpson, or Mrs., or whatever you are. I don't mean to be rude, but I listened in on the extension when my daughter called you yesterday. And I am very upset. What causes it? Is it because somebody molests you when you were young? My husband thinks it's because somebody molested her when she was young. I mean, what can a woman do for another woman? You know, a man can support her. I want her to live a normal life.

RUTH: Like listening in on her daughter's phone calls? I am sorry you are upset, but let's slow down and try to get some answers to some of your questions.

CALLER: Well, I want you to stay away from my daughter.

RUTH: Just a moment—your daughter called me, out of fear and confusion. You heard our conversation. She had

23

better talk to someone who has some facts about homosexuality rather than all of this misinformation. I am very happily placed in a beautiful and solid relationship, and I have no interest in your daughter other than as a human being who needs help and whom maybe I can help.

CALLER: Well, you don't sound like a man, but don't women like you try to dress like men?

At this point I told her that I would answer her questions, which I had been trying to keep track of in my homemade type of shorthand. I explained a number of the things which were dealt with in the first chapter. Alicia's mother seemed to begin to listen and apologized for having been rude. She said that she was very worried, that she didn't want Alicia to "molest somebody in a restaurant. I mean she is very cute—my daughter is very cute and feminine. And I don't want my daughter in that sort of life. But thank you." Alicia's mother then hung up.

The next day Alicia called, nearly hysterical, to apologize and to find out what her mother had said to me. We talked for a while. There had been a confrontation between Alicia and her parents. I told her that her mother just does not understand her situation, and that it is not necessarily her mother's fault that she doesn't. I explained that there is no place for parents to turn for information and that it is our society which makes us all victims of fear. Alicia said that she just had to get away from the constant pressure and the fights in her home. She didn't understand how I could talk to her and try to help her after the call from her mother. I told her not to worry about that at all, that I am used to handling difficult situations. Similar bigotry and fears have been expressed to me many times.

24

Alicia said that she would call me after she "got herself together."

Some days later I received another call from Alicia's mother. She wanted to know if I had seen her daughter or heard from her—that she had left home. I told her about Alicia's call of apology but said that I had no idea where Alicia might be. She said that her husband wanted to call the police and send them after her, that, after all, she was "one of those sickies." I told her not to call the police, that it would be terrible to be responsible for having a homosexual charge placed on her daughter's record.

During our long conversation she expressed great concern about her husband's cruelty to her daughter. She said that he was very difficult to control. Somehow, she said, she would keep him from calling the police. We talked about various aspects of homosexuality and the role expected of women in general. She asked if I thought she should go to some of the gay bars and try to find Alicia. We decided that it would be best if she waited to hear from Alicia, and agreed that when she did she would express her understanding of her daughter's sexual identity.

I did not hear from either of them again, but perhaps they will be able to work out their individual lives with some dignity and compassion for each other.

I give this detailed account of Alicia's experience to illustrate the full impact of the family problems surrounding the homosexual child.

It is true that in a few cases parents and relatives of young lesbians have been surprisingly good in their adjustment to and ultimate acceptance and support of their daughters. A specific example is Ellen Povill's family. Ellen decided when she turned eighteen that she was no longer capable of tolerating the pressure to get a boyfriend and the other pressures common in practically every home where a girl is growing to womanhood; she made up her mind to tell her family about her lesbianism.

This is an honest and personally courageous decision which not many lesbians are able to make for themselves, because too often the lesbian is put off by the many terrible things she hears. Ellen has told young women at D.O.B. that if they find the strength to tell their parents at age eighteen, they can expect to re-establish good relationships with them, even the most conservative types, within several years, during which time "they simply get used to the idea."

She advises that a young lesbian can lose her family for good in a poor and deceptive relationship, unless she makes her identity clear in as positive an explanation as possible —and then she must not be deterred from that identity. According to Ellen, "Of course, when I told my family, I was already living away from home. This is difficult, but if women would tell their families when they are eighteen, contact is gradually restored, and within a few years you are accepted again as your own person. Actually, I am closer to my mother now than I was before I told her. There is a good chance that the response to a young lesbian's honesty will be: 'Get out of the house'; but it's worth it because you have your own life to live whether your family accepts you or not."

Ellen's father took the news of her sexual orientation with extreme difficulty; her mother was very distressed the day Ellen told her, but later was able to discuss the "problem" with equity and understanding. She no longer regards it as a problem. Other relatives gradually reached the point where they could accept Ellen and her homosexual women friends as full-fledged family members.

26

Some of Ellen's high school friends did not have the same luck with their families, however. When Ellen went to a gay bar for the first time, she saw many of her high school friends there. Two sisters who were lesbians and who were living with an alcoholic father had a serious problem—when they told their father, he announced that they would have to stay locked up at home, that they could not go out, except to school, until they were able to go out with boys. Ellen and her friends explained the problem to homosexual young men they knew and a group of homosexuals, both boys and girls, came to the house. The sisters were then allowed to go out because they were going out on a "normal date with boys."

"Locking" lesbian girls into the home is a rather common reaction. The parents feel that as long as the child can't get out, she will "come to her senses and change." This, of course, doesn't happen. She will only come to a point of neurosis, rejection, and alienation from the prison-family she is forced to live with.

A certain portion of the lesbian population seems to have been born of parents with chronic high blood pressure and/or heart ailments. Many lesbians have been saying for years that they can't possibly tell their parents because the father has high blood pressure and the mother has a heart condition, and it "would just kill them to find out that I am a lesbian." It is amazing how many young women have such a devastated image of their identity that it actually breeds fear of fatality for their parents. Many lesbians who are closeted give this reason for not wanting, or being unable, to come out.

Another reason given is that a grandmother or aunt or other relative is "too old to take the shock." Often the elderly relative lives very happily many full years and the lesbian spends these years developing the closet habit which she usually never breaks.

The case of a young D.O.B. woman contradicts this "too old to tell" theory. She decided to tell her grandmother. Her grandmother constantly pressed her with, "Some day you'll meet a nice doctor or nice lawyer" whenever the young woman answered "When are you going to marry?" with "I just haven't met anyone I want to marry." The young woman—she was eighteen at the time—finally told her grandmother that she wasn't going to marry because she was a lesbian. The grandmother patted her hand and said, "Don't worry, some day you will meet a nice doctor or nice lawyer." The woman said, "Grandma, didn't you hear what I said?" The grandmother said, "All right, so some day you will meet a nice lady doctor or a nice lady lawyer. . . ." The grandmother and the young woman are good family friends today.

The most typical story, however, is somewhat different. When Ellen Povill was vice-president of D.O.B., a young woman wrote to her. (At this time D.O.B. had a referral service in psychiatric, medical, and religious areas, and we were constantly receiving requests for information and help.) The following quotes are excerpted from a letter written in early April 1971:

> Dear Ellen,
> It was very kind of you to suggest that I call and speak with you. However, someone is always home in my house. . . . Would you mind if I do call you when I'm feeling down and everything looks hopeless? It happens quite often and I need someone to talk to. You would think that at age 21 I would be able to handle my emotional turmoils. Maybe when I finally "come out" all the way, things will be better emotionally. . . .

28

I'm really upset that I can't come to City College next
week [Ellen and I were to lecture at the college]. . . .
I hope you don't object to my writing to and confiding
in you. I know you understand the plight of a lonely,
"closeted" lesbian.

> Thank you so much,
> [Signature]

P.S. I'm sorry that I have to write long-hand, but if I
start to type someone always wants to know what I'm
doing. If you write back could it be done in a plain envelope without a return address?

> again, thanks.

The following excerpts are from a letter of October 1971
from the same woman.

Dear Ellen,
I have written to you several times about my problem.
Now I am looking for a psychiatrist who deals specifi-
cally with homosexuals. I am desperate.
Please send me some names immediately. I understand
you do know psychiatrists. Even though I am not a
member of D.O.B. I implore your help in this matter.
Thank you very much.

> Sincerely,
> [Signature]

P.S. As usual, send it in a plain envelope with no mention of my problem in the letter. My mother opens my
mail and reads it. I need a psychiatrist to get over this
hang up I have and to stop feeling guilty.

Ellen called the young woman and referred her to one
of the D.O.B. psychiatrists, a woman who has helped many
lesbians with family problems. Since that time the young
lesbian has consulted with the doctor, moved away from her
oppressive family situation, and is now able to live free from

the deception and anxieties which were destroying her. Her parents still do not know, or at least have not acknowledged, that she is a lesbian.

There are endless stories similar to these. There are a number of extremely ugly instances of girls and young women being badly beaten by their fathers who learned of their homosexuality. In one case, a father stood at the top of the stairs in his home and threw large, heavy construction nuts and bolts from his workshop at his daughter, screaming "Freak!" at her. He beat her several times, not telling her why. It was only later that the girl found out that a "well-meaning friend" had told her father that she was a lesbian.

Parents who think that their daughter or son might be homosexual should talk about it in a nonjudgmental way to their child. They should *ask* rather than provide the answers; their child can probably give them more cogent information on the subject than can the "family doctor."

The larger part of the burden of providing security, comfort, and love in a parent-child relationship logically should rest with the parent. That a child is homosexual does not make the parent retroactively "unfit"; a parent of a homosexual child becomes unfit, in the true sense of the word, only if ignorance and prejudice drive the parent to ignore or degrade the homosexual child. Since homosexuality is a natural and loving state, rejection, or false compassion and understanding in an attempt to "convert" the child to heterosexuality, is ridiculous and harmful. These parental attitudes may permanently destroy relationships with the homosexual child.

Some have said that it might be better if one were given the option of picking one's family and being born to one's friends. One has the shifting tapestry of friends for most of a lifetime. Family is arbitrarily put on us and there it sits, for most of us, until we are of age.

If a parent should be understanding and sympathetic, the young homosexual should at the soonest time possible openly state her identity, simply because it *is* her identity, no matter how she may try to submerge it. When it is made, the statement should be as gently firm as possible. She may expect anything from a family explosion to quiet acceptance to total rejection. Time is cited as the element which will heal all things (one should not be fooled, however, when told that time will "heal" homosexuality—it will take the same amount of time to "heal" homosexuality as it will to "heal" the parents' heterosexuality).

Honesty cannot be offered to the relationship with parents in most cases, however, until the age of consent, unless the young lesbian is prepared for the possibility of her parents' take-over of her human rights. Some parents have been known to be wonderful—most, however, have been bad to impossible. Each person must judge her own situation. I know that the years seem longer when one is younger, and that a year or two or three can seem endless; but if the lesbian has doubts about her parents' response to her homosexuality, she should wait until she is of age. She is dealing with the rest of her life. It would be far better to live it in a reasonable relationship with her parents if it is possible. It is immeasurably better to live it without the scars of the forced and often hysterical family conferences with psychiatrists and clergymen which could possibly be the outcome of a premature honesty.

Of equal importance: the heterosexual child should try to be open as well, despite dishonest and slanted sex education which tends to lead a child to archaic attitudes about homosexuality. Should she (or he) learn that a mother or

31

father is homosexual, the child should try very hard not to let the myth-wishes about us allow her to be exploited against her own parent or parents and her homosexual peers through unintelligent and unjust attitudes.

Despite the pressures, both psychic and physical, brought to bear on their daughters by so many families, the young women persist in their natural sexual preferences. The scars which so many lesbian women currently carry are not because of their homosexuality; they were caused instead by the abrasive values the microcosmic family has inherited from our macrocosmic society.

3

Social Attitudes
Stay in Line
or Lose Your Place
in the Pecking Order

Social scarring of the homosexual is post-familial; it develops as a layer over the abrasions incurred in getting into and, it is hoped, out of the family closet.

Bigotry toward lesbians comes from all quarters, some of them unexpected. It is naturally almost always more overt and cruel when manifested in relation to a self-avowed lesbian. Here are a few random examples:

• Two young lesbian acquaintances were upset because they were having problems with one of the women's parents. During this period of upheaval in their young lives, one of the women discovered a lump in her breast and was certain it was cancer. She told her friend that she saw no point in going on if she had cancer, and in her depression over her health crisis she talked of suicide. Her friend called Manhattan Suicide Prevention to get help. A woman at the organization who identified herself only as "Kay" asked for the "total story." When she was told that the women were lesbians, she said, "Oh, you're lesbians? Well, you got her into this; you can get her out of it!" And hung up.

• When I told a businesswoman friend of more than six years that I am lesbian, her response was: "Surely you have made a mistake. You have always been so feminine. No, I'm sorry to say I just don't believe it." Our relationship, despite its previous warmth, has become literally nonexistent.

• A young woman in the emergency clinic of New York's Bellevue Hospital was being examined by a neurologist for unexplained blackouts she had been having (before going to the hospital she had been told that her blood sugar was low). The neurologist during his long interview was told that she was homosexual. "Oh, then I know what's wrong with you," he said. "You need to get laid by a man."

• A friend of many years standing who "respected" my lesbianism expressed doubt about my views on practically everything else we ever discussed. She said that even though I am, what she termed, a "natural" lesbian, I am prone to relate everything to my sexuality, e.g. ecology: "You think that not having children is the answer to everything." (We were discussing overconsumption of natural resources.) Civil rights: "How can you relate homosexuality to the civil-rights fight—there is no connection." Feminism: "Don't be ridiculous—*women* women just don't feel that way." Abortion: "You can't talk about religion as an oppressor of women— that is your view as a lesbian."

• I got into the subway following a demonstration and was wearing a lesbian button. Two women followed me onto the train and sat beside me. This was during the height of the button-wearing period, so one of them leaned forward and read mine. She jumped up saying, "I won't sit next to you!" I smiled and said, "It's not contagious, you know." For some inexplicable reason she started hitting at me saying, "You can't talk that way about my husband." I still cannot fathom what that meant. I stood and tried to take hold of her wrists to stop the stupidity. With this, her friend started hitting at me saying, "Take your hands off her, you queer!" At this point a man who had been sitting at the far end of the train came to us and said, "Come on. Let's cut it out." The women stood back and the first woman pointed at me, saying to the man, "But she's a queer—look, look, she's a *pervert!*" The man looked at my button and said, "If I'd known that I wouldn't have stopped you."

Since our society is built on the man-woman roles being kept in balance, which is to say, *out* of balance, anything that seems to threaten the supervalue placed on "manhood" is deemed unacceptable. Anything that detracts from our society's emphasis on "femininity" (such as women operating from any power-based autonomy) is immediately suspect. And since the socially derogatory label of "lesbian" is applied to any woman who seems to function outside the limits of "femininity," *all* women, not just lesbians, are potentially subject to the oppression of women via the oppression of lesbians.

In our culture a high price is placed on "femininity" and all the "wiles" involved in its practice. "Femininity" is a big business. The concept of lesbianism threatens this business because, no matter how "feminine" a lesbian might be, she represents a threat to the "game plan."

Am I exaggerating? Let me quote from an August 6, 1972, article in *The New York Times,* "The Secret Power of Femininity."

35

Stand before a mirror in the privacy of your room and say to yourself, "I am just a helpless woman at the mercy of you big, strong men." . . . Stand before the mirror and say to yourself, "I expect you to pamper and humor me." With this thought in mind, try a pretty pout, stick out your lower lip as much as to say, "I thought you liked me." . . . After perfecting this before the mirror, practice this exercise upon every man you meet. . . . You must drop every suggestion in speech, apparel and manner that you are able to . . . take care of your own affairs.

Maurine and Elbert Startup, the authors, also write this advice to young women:

Shaking hands is an art for the feminine woman. She will begin eagerly and confidingly, then suddenly seem to realize it is a man's hand she is holding, and begin shyly drawing her own hand away. . . . Nothing can be better designed to remind the man immediately of the contrast of her feminine shyness with his manly thought-lessness and indifference. [What is manly about thought-lessness and indifference, I wonder.]

The Startups emphasize their conviction that our great-grandmothers knew a thing or two when it came to charming members of the opposite sex and that *"wiles could still pay off handsomely"* (author's italics).

Apparently there are a great number of women who accept this willful deceptiveness as "femininity," since the Startups are earning approximately $75,000 from their Femininity Forums, twelve sessions of three hours each, for which 250 young women each pay $300. According to the *Times*, "These weren't the first classes and they won't be the last. Daughters of women who once attended the forums are now beginning to sign up for them."

When our society can make such caricatures of women,

36

it is small wonder that so many need some consciousness-raising. But consciousness-raising, it should be remembered, is only a method of getting people *ready* to enter a movement; it is not the movement itself. This is the mistake in appraisal that many make. Consciousness-raising has become a socially acceptable concept, but it keeps people at the talking stage . . . safely in conversation in their own living rooms, confronting their sisters or brothers, and themselves: but not the external oppressors. Where real consciousness is raised is in the streets, at action demonstrations, dealing with cops who brutalize, and in the courts. Those in consciousness-raising groups should constantly bear in mind that their group is a means and not an end.

As president of D.O.B., New York, I received a number of hate-letters, all anonymous. Unable to attack the source of his own oppression and fear, the writer of the anonymous hate-letter aims his frustration, fear, and hostility at those he believes to be lower in the pecking order. He is safe because he cannot be held responsible for his action. Following are excerpts from a five-page letter sent to me (this was one of many similar letters):

> [The letter writer is referring to the article that appeared in *The New York Times Magazine,* "The Disciples of Sappho, Updated" by Judy Klemesrud.]
> This is one of the most vormit news items I seen yet put out by the communist puppets to disgrace the American way of life. . . . God created man and the man is always on top, he is boss. God Country, nature says so. God created MAN to serve him, and a woman to serve man. . . . Why do you think you dress against society, Because you'll all trying to attract not women   men. Deep down inside you all know it no women no matter who she may be rich or strong can compare to a man, no women on earth can compete with a man for jobs, sex anything! You and all youre shit faced women are

nothing but hand me downs, sore loses, malajusted freaks, biological mistakes and child rapers. . . . Sure you and your kind have rights, rights to parade into the nearest mental camp and stay there till every breath and thought of homosexuality is wiped from the face of the earth.

The reason we have drug addiction, V.D., hippies yippies and Manson types is all the shit of the communist and the communist puppets the niggers and the fags, both men and women queers . . . the REAL American who worked all his life never been on welfare . . . *has* to live and work and put up with the niggers, now the fags? Oh, no baby it enough with the niggers never, ever, the fags, it just is never going to happen. . . .

Sincerely,
A defender of the real life, love,
and courage of the American peoples.
B'klyn, N. Y.

The first reading of this letter has such shock value that an immediate appraisal of its content is perhaps impossible. The distillation of obscenity and hate, in "defense" of decency and "the real life, love and courage," is so intense that the first impulse is to push it away from the consciousness as too ugly and sick to be credited; however, this letter contains, in concentrated form, the fears and bigotry that haunt many people to a lesser degree—many who use nicer words or no words at all. Hate-letter writers are relegated to the "isolated nut" category, but there are too many of them around to disregard them totally. Theirs is but the extreme reflection of how far too many "normal, decent" people feel about those who are different.

With this base of ethnocentrism, the alien characteristics of all groups other than his own often become one in the mind of the bigot. These characteristics may all be different, but they represent a collective, single threat.

One example of this is shown by the findings of a major, two-year-long, $425,000 Lutheran Church research project. The report on their study of Lutheranism in the United States found that anti-Semitism "is not a separate entity, but just one facet of generalized prejudice." About one in five American Lutherans were found to have anti-Semitic attitudes. Two in every five tended to reject persons different from themselves in life styles, values, and beliefs—"especially homosexuals, drug addicts, Communists and hippies." Dr. Arthur P. Johnson, a University of Minnesota sociologist who was a member of the Lutheran Study research team, explains that the roots of prejudice are multi-dimensional and are linked with rigid personalities threatened by change or diversity.

The Archie Bunker phenomenon illustrates such bigotry on an even broader level. It is said by devotees of the television program that anybody who doesn't like Archie is some kind of humorless grouch. And yet the entire concept of the program is built on hate and bigotry; it introduces the worst of degrading labels—kike, fag, spic, chink, etc. Those who champion the show say that "Archie really got his this week," that he really was leveled by a member of whatever group was under attack during the specific "entertainment" period.

The "All in a Family" homosexual episode, for instance, had to do with a "fag" who happened to be a football coach. In this case, the person who bested Archie was the exception—this is true in practically every episode. It is the *exceptional* "fag" (that is, exceptional in Archie's values) who wins out. The door is open for continued prejudice against the rest of the groups, which Archie still loathes, *as a group*. Let that "fag" be a peace demonstrator, a leader in the gay movement, a designer, or a hairdresser, and he would not find his way into any Archie Bunker script. The show is based in generalized prejudice; that it enjoys such widespread popularity is a devastating comment on the bigotry abroad in this country.

This bigotry is built into the system to keep minorities separate from one another; it is manipulated to keep too many people from being too discontent for too long; it also makes a broad-spectrum coalition impossible, since each group has learned anything from distrust of to hatred for all other groups.

To translate this from an abstract concept into a real-life situation, let's examine one of many instances:

Just a few years ago, many workers in the automotive and construction industries were the most vocal on the issue of welfare. Those on welfare were "bums" or "millionaires," depending on the point of view of the myth-teller. Poor marches and welfare-rights demonstrations were called "commie-inspired" and were considered un-American, being "against the work ethic." Hostilities were built between the two groups of people; these hostilities will be felt for a long time. And yet, in a very short time, those same workers have been forced into a welfare condition—*their* group had to be manipulated to a lower rung on the ladder in order to support the oil and other related industries. They will learn that one doesn't get rich by going on welfare. But class memories are short, and self-concern is persistent, and instead of a possible future coalition of the two groups, they will probably be held in place in the cultural pecking order. If not, their threat to government, and its power via the corporate-military complex, would be too great.

Had the workers examined the myths they babbled so recently and found them to be invalid, they could have joined forces with the poor to change conditions and secure

40

their future work situation. But they were too happy with their "position" in society to realize at the time that they also were an exploitable segment of the population. This is just one example of the pecking order at work.

Far down in the social pecking order is the lesbian, about whom so little is really known. Often otherwise relatively enlightened people still cling to the negative clichés about lesbians.

There is very little that each individual can do about changing attitudes of a society except to speak out against bigotry in any way possible. Too often someone in any given group will say something negative about another group, assuming automatically that all those present agree. And too often those present let it slide, either for their own personal or political "advancement," or because they don't want to argue. We should never allow others to co-opt our minds and hearts, since we have ethical and intellectual obligations to integrity. We are responsible for our own opinions and thoughts, formed, we hope, from fact and not myth, and we should not allow ourselves to lose these opinions by default.

Many people believe, since there is so much talk about homosexuality today, that great progress has been made in establishing civil rights for homosexuals. Too seldom do they analyze what is being said in terms of basic human values. For instance, I have heard people say, "I saw a lesbian on television—isn't that wonderful? Ten years ago, that would never have happened." This is true; however, I saw the lesbian too. She said, when asked by a CBS reporter why she was involved in street theater in celebration of the anniversary of woman's suffrage, "Oh, I'm just out here to show that being a lesbian really isn't so bad. Actually being a

41

lesbian is fun. . . ." Keep in mind that this was a "lesbian leader" speaking. Self-acceptance is not enough! Imagine an Angela Davis making the statement: "Being a black really isn't so bad." Even when people hear minority movement "spokespeople" they should take the time to think carefully about what is being said, applying the words to their own minority or a minority to which they are sympathetic. Our social apathy is in part caused by accepting myths for fact, by accepting talk for action.

True, there is "talk" about homosexuality. But it is going to take *more* talk, and more than *just* talk before the lesbian is understood and given her civil rights. In the meantime, lesbianism is used as a "scare tactic" label for any woman who wishes to confront and end her oppression. It is a sword of Damocles poised over the head of every woman.

4

Lesbianism and Feminism
A Connection?
Don't Ask "Women's Lib"

> *Lesbianism has been a difficult issue in the [feminist]*
> *movement. Many feminists believe that lesbians should*
> *have the same status as all other feminists, but other*
> *women have been wary of lesbianism becoming too*
> *closely identified with the movement in the public*
> *consciousness.*
> —The New York Times, *August 22, 1972*

Whether it's called public consciousness or societal attitudes or something else altogether, the response to any member of an oppressed group who steps out of her closet of
oppression and takes a sp toward freedom is that that
person is suddenly suspect. If the oppressed wait for public
consciousness and attitudes to change before they open the
door, they will remain oppressed for a long time to come.
This has been amply demonstrated in the women's movement.

Those who have been in the movement for any length of
time are aware that probably the only true political theorist it has produced is Ti-Grace Atkinson. At the outset of
this latest feminist movement, it was she who posited that
women, as a class, should function for the good of all
women. It was she who first took a position on abortion in

the early days of NOW—and her sisters regarded her as some kind of radical nut. "We just don't talk about such things as abortion—the public isn't ready for it." Ti-Grace made a statement on lesbianism, and the cry went up: "There goes crazy Ti-Grace!" Her position on prostitution sent women scurrying for their closets. "What will the women in the hinterlands think?" Two years or more following each statement, the "movement" seems to catch up with Ti-Grace. But in the beginning, the attitude was that the women in the movement couldn't possibly ally themselves with women who needed abortions—nice ladies didn't get pregnant if they weren't married, and if they were married, they didn't admit that they chose not to have children; prostitutes just weren't nice ladies, or they wouldn't go into that kind of work (the most vocal on this subject were those whom Florynce Kennedy refers to as "split-level prostitutes," women who become dehumanized in oppressive marriages because they are married to good providers who take care of all the bills); lesbians? well, they aren't ladies at all; they are queers, and since we are already being accused of being lesbians, we can't consider *them* as allies.

During this time, a few lesbians in NOW who were closeted were more often than not the conservatives of NOW. It was all right for lesbians to work for the movement, but they were never to acknowledge that they were lesbian, or attempt to cross over into the gay movement (there were actually lesbians in NOW who used different names in D.O.B.). An idea of how the women's movement regarded lesbians is shown by this excerpt from an article Ti-Grace wrote for the May 1971 D.O.B. Newsletter:

> I was a member of NOW's New York chapter from its beginning in February 1967 until my resignation as

president of New York NOW in October 1968. Lesbianism, as a political issue, has had a curious history in the Women's Movement (including NOW) in that the issue has been raised primarily in terms of rejecting male-female relationships. Lesbianism, within feminism, has been *perceived* more as anti-male than pro-female.

From its inception, NOW's slogan appearing on its stationery masthead has been: "Full equality for women in truly equal partnership with men." This slogan always disturbed me, because it seemed to suggest that justice for women was reasonable insofar as it was inoffensive to men. While I had nothing against men at the onset of feminism, this slogan included what seemed to me an uncomfortable "rider." Lesbianism in NOW, as well as the rest of the Movement, has stood for pushing men on feminism past some desirable point (to be defined by men), so that women (as individuals) might risk losing their men. The premise here is that women *need* men in some metaphysical sense. Thus, "separatism" was "lesbianism," attacks on institutions locking in individuals on a cross-sexual basis, such as marriage, family, prostitution, rape, pornography, were expressions of lesbianism, questioning vaginal orgasm was lesbianism . . . Raising the issue of whether men should be at all meetings was lesbianism. . . .

Ti-Grace went on to tell how she was approached by a lesbian at the opening of the D.O.B. Lesbian Center in January of 1971. She was asked to take part in a "coup" in NOW with lesbianism as a focal issue. She replied: "Who wants NOW?" She disagreed with NOW on *many* issues; lesbianism was only one of them. In addition, the women planning the coup were among those who were Ti-Grace's strongest opponents. It did not occur to Ti-Grace to inform any NOW people—even those she ran into from time to time —on the lesbian-issue plan. Apparently the "coup" group had entrusted many if not all the lesbians in NOW with the

45

plan. Two closeted lesbian NOW members informed on their lesbian "sisters" to the conservative faction, which included the bulk of the men members of NOW. One of the men told Ti-Grace that without this advance information the victory of the conservatives would have been far from certain. As Ti-Grace wrote later in the D.O.B. Newsletter, "This is not new to resistance movements, but it is time that people understand that such betrayals will have to be lived with publicly."

New York NOW has refused to make a supportive statement on lesbianism because "the rest of the country, the suburban housewives are not ready for it."

Despite this pandering to the "public consciousness" on the part of its New York Chapter, the national NOW has issued a resolution in favor of lesbian rights. As of late 1974, New York NOW has failed to follow suit. It has also absented itself from the long battle to pass a law against discrimination against homosexuals in New York City. It has taken no organizational stand on the issue.

Obviously, New York NOW and other parts of the women's movement are fooling themselves and others; its split personality on ethics and principles has been developed out of fear and lack of political responsibility.

When expressed *outside* one's own group, a statement against prejudice becomes a responsible political act. Silence on such an issue helps foster oppression of all minority groups. The "puritan ethic" of the great majority in the women's movement has seriously retarded understanding of and intelligent coping with such prejudice.

Today, women have become increasingly aware that something is wrong with their lives. Many of them, so heavily into role-playing and working within the accepted authority of a male-oriented society, have begun to decide that alternate life styles might be valid. Some women have said that the more they examined the resentment they felt toward their oppressive relationships with men the more they thought it might be possible to "try a woman." Some women have said in open forum that as they articulated hostility toward the men in their lives, they were "turned on" by women. Often, however, these women were functioning within the framework of their conditioned female role, not having gotten to the root of their oppression at all. Such women often regard the lesbian as the "aggressor"—they superimpose their societal attitudes on the "alternative relationship" and transfer the "male" role to the lesbian. There always have been, and probably always will be, some lesbian relationships which are oppressive to one or both of the women involved. Usually in such instances this is because the women have been indoctrinated by the cultural concept of role-play—*it* is "normal," and by adopting it, they will be setting up a life acceptable by all the standards they have ever learned. There are even a few lesbians who regard the feminist movement as politically ridiculous. This probably stems from a feeling that feminism threatens their "aggressor" position in the personal hierarchy of their own relationships. Such lesbians, and the heterosexual women previously described, are in a political sense almost identical in outlook. They are usually unable to cope with the responsibility of a mutually equal relationship.

One-to-one, or for that matter multiple, relationships are rarely equal in the true sense of the word. Equality is talked about endlessly, is held aloft as the standard, and yet the simplest social structure, the one-to-one relationship, is generally a reflection of myths and myth-wishes. It is supposed to be a power play, one the "lover" and one the "loved." Think of some of the time-worn platitudes: if jeal-

47

ousy is not shown by a love partner then how can one be sure of the love; fights are a natural part of a love relationship; the first hundred years are the hardest; people have to have disagreements so they can "kiss and make up," alleged by some to be their happiest moments. There are few relationships in which mutual trust, freedom, and equality really exist, in which both partners accept and accommodate *both* needs in themselves and each other. The cultural model is the heterosexual marriage, a relationship not especially noted for equality. Therefore, many people do not *expect* to find this quality in a relationship and accept its absence as "normal."

Sometimes "women's movement" women think they will "try" a lesbian as an "alternative," or for "kicks," or to "really liberate themselves sexually." These are all expressions which I and other lesbians have heard women use. It is fairly clear, however, that they are exploiting lesbians as a group. Counterpart sexism is employed by the heterosexual woman who assumes that since lesbians love women they will love her. Of course, these women have come one step closer to understanding lesbianism, it is true: they at least regard a lesbian as someone who experiences a positive, rather than a negative, role in life. But such women impose the concept of the "woman" on themselves, and their sexual partner therefore must be the "other," the non-woman. What many women don't realize is that the word homosexual comes not from the Latin, *homo,* meaning "man," but rather from the Greek, *homos,* meaning "the same." Many lesbians do not regard their lesbianism as a sexual-emotional counterpoint to being a woman; on the contrary, it is one and the same. This is why homosexual relationships have the *potential* for equality. Since more and more homosexuals are stating their identity and growing away from thinking, working, and living within the confines and values of the heterosexual culture, an increasing number of us have realized that anyone, woman or man, who exploits us as "a different kind of sex object" is ultimately going to have some explaining to do, not only to us but to themselves. Such people are dragging along behind them the oppressive role-play of a society we have left.

There are some feminists who do not exploit lesbians, who regard us as women, as sisters, as total human beings who need no excuses, no explanations, no reasons. These women, insofar as feminism may be connected with lesbianism, in some instances share the same autonomy of being unhindered by the financial need for men. They make a decision for self-determination and usually live by it; similarly, the lesbian has to make her way through life exclusive of the support of a male partner, a feminist course to take. However, autonomy is not the crux of the issue.

The relationship between feminism and lesbianism is tenuous at best. Being a feminist is by its very nature being a political animal; being a lesbian is political insofar as a lesbian's life does take on in certain respects the *modus operandi* of the feminist's life. However, being a lesbian does not necessarily mean being a political animal, any more than being black connotes a political orientation. Many lesbians are not active politically, nor do they wish to be. Some of those in the movement are pretty good feminists; others are not. At the same time, there are many heterosexual women who call themselves feminists who are not, in the true sense of the word. So in a pure sense there is no shared link of a political nature between the lesbian and feminist movements as they function today; other, of course, than that both the feminist and the lesbian give their concern, attention, and energy to women.

I used to believe that lesbians were the pioneers in the feminist movement, until I saw where we stood and still stand in that movement. I also thought that we were the political avant-garde of the women's movement, until I experienced the lack of political respect we lesbians show one another. This lack of respect is anti-feminist, anti-lesbian, and anti-human. A lesbian can be an oppressor of women—in fact, one well-known lesbian writer once suggested les-·bian whorehouses for women. What could be more anti-feminist?

There have been many definitions of lesbianism by homosexuals, by heterosexuals, by all sorts of people; there have been many descriptions of what a lesbian life is supposed to be like, what it means to the lesbian herself. Usually these definitions and descriptions differ quite radically. My personal—which is also my political—appraisal of lesbianism is that it is a love relationship between women of equal status, of equal trust, of equal freedom to pursue their lives individually and together. It is also a way of life which has as its natural concomitant concern for all women and their attendant problems. There might be a number of lesbians who agree with this definition politically but who do not or cannot live a personal life which reflects this definition of lesbianism. Such a life is seldom available to many of us, because we are all carrying around the scars of oppression and the rules of the heterosexual culture.

In the sense of women supporting women in both the personal and political goals of freedom, there could and certainly should be a connection between feminism and lesbianism. This connection, however, has been rendered faulty because of the hostility which exists toward the lesbian as a sub-class within the class of women and because of the resultant negative lesbian reaction to this hostility.

There is a tremendous amount of horizontal hostility among all women, and small wonder. It is a natural by-product of oppression; it is part of the pathology. This hostility exists among heterosexual women, among homosexual women, between the two groups of women, and among groups of women from various ethnic backgrounds. This hostility represents the fear of the oppressed, just as bigotry is based on fear of the alien. Such hostility and fear have been responsible for the fragmentation of a number of women's organizations. They are also the reasons for the reluctance of the women's movement to consider seriously, et alone work toward, true coalition. If the movement were serious, hostility would abate and, it is hoped, be turned away from ourselves and toward the external oppressors. We might even develop a conscience for the women's movement. We don't have one now. We need women in the movement who realize how destructive self-contempt directed at any group of women can be. But so often many "feminists" are the first to exploit the oppression of lesbians as a group, and the last to take any sort of strong position in support of lesbians' rights to full citizenship in the community of women.

There are women in the movement who believe that this situation has changed and that feminists and lesbians are working together politically. There is some rather hard-core evidence to the contrary. Late in 1974 I spoke at New York NOW on political lesbianism. The board member of NOW present was not aware that lesbians are "extra-legal," and she had not even heard that a gay-civil-rights bill had been considered and defeated by the New York City Council. At the same time, a few of the lesbians there said that NOW really was good on the lesbian issue, that "women there accept us and even put their arm around you, and really make

51

you feel welcome." Personal acceptance is nice, but it is not enough.

In February of 1975 I spoke on a panel on "Lesbianism and the Law" at an all-day feminist workshop. Held at Columbia Law School, organized by New York City Metropolitan Law Women, with a keynote address by New York Congresswoman Bella Abzug, the panels covered all aspects of feminism. The moderator for the lesbian panel introduced the panel by saying, "There was a hassle about this panel—a lot of the women thought the issue might be offensive, but we set it up anyway." There are other similar examples too numerous and repetitive to list here.

The long record of the women's movement's hostility toward lesbianism has resulted in some instances in returned hostilities of lesbians toward the women's movement. That the hostility is justified in many instances does not justify some of the anti-feminist attitudes which have developed in the lesbian community. We have the dyke-separatist mentality, the all-women-are-lesbians attitude, the you-are-not-a-true-feminist-unless-you-are-a-lesbian nonsense. These are all destructive and alienating attitudes; perhaps even more important, they are neither very bright nor realistic. The few lesbians who hold such views certainly think of themselves as militants. They are not—they are politically naive and irresponsible. They are not going to perform any tangible act to free the lesbian from oppression or to promote movement coalition. The only forceful method for accomplishing change is working toward a movement coalition, not separating women off into smaller and smaller groups which work in opposition to each other.

The feminist movement women who are heterosexual must work toward changing their own prejudices and attitudes about lesbians. Their basic fears about lesbianism must be worked out. Because these fears do exist.

Lesbians who refuse to regard abortion or divorce as their issues, since they are "not lesbian issues," are totally unrealistic, since there are so many lesbian mothers and lesbian ex-wives who have gone through the nightmare of custody and divorce battles. Lesbians who have such views are as irresponsible to their class—women—as are the heterosexual women in the movement who refuse to fight for lesbian rights. Lesbian rights are a vital issue to the women's movement, and to believe otherwise is to betray the bond (which I *sometimes* think is mythical) we all share.

Fear of the unknown is the most difficult problem the bigot has to overcome. Some heterosexual women are trying to work toward intelligent understanding about us; meanwhile, hostilities are piling up between us. There is talk of excluding lesbians from some feminist groups. There is talk of excluding heterosexual women from some lesbian groups. This sort of fragmentation with its attendant publicity is precisely the sort of thing the system wants. Women must get themselves together as a class and not allow the disruptive, the fearful, the reactionary among them to detract from their collective goal of total freedom. We have the numbers, but we must re-channel the energies now being consumed by hostilities into positive political actions. Until this is done, no movement—including the women's and the lesbian movements—will be able to accomplish its goals.

Bella Abzug has made a very strong and supportive statement on homosexual rights. She is dynamic and certainly one of the first women from among the Women's Political Caucus leaders to speak out for homosexuals in firm, no-

nonsense terms and I am confident that she would have been appalled at the introduction of the Columbia panel on lesbianism. Shirley Chisholm is another; she has also made statements on the subject which must have shaken the Betty Friedans of the movement. It is one thing to make statements within the confined context of a particular event, such as the press conference the women's movement held in response to the *Time* magazine attack on Kate Millett and the women's movement in general, following Kate's announcement that she is bisexual. It is another thing altogether in the overall context of women's rights for leaders of the movement to include lesbianism as an issue as a matter of course, in a way which assumes that lesbian rights are a real concern to the movement.

It is only when the movement reaches the point that its leaders automatically include lesbian rights as one of its natural and positive goals that lesbians as a class will be full-fledged members of the women's movement.

Where are the lesbian representatives in the Women's Political Caucus? I mean the self-avowed politically committed movement lesbian who could speak with an overall understanding for the great number of lesbian women in the country? She is not visible as of now. Nor was the women's movement visible during or after the incredibly insulting episode at the last National Democratic Convention in which the minority plank for homosexual rights was sent down to ignominious defeat. Hardly anybody, except probably homosexuals, watched far into the early morning to see the pitiable treatment the homosexual rights plank received. Just before it was roundly defeated, a woman delegate spoke against it, saying that the plank should be defeated "to save the morals of our children." Vote. Defeat. Finally another woman delegate managed to get the floor

and objected to the offensive remarks made about those homosexuals who spoke in behalf of the plank and about all
homosexuals. Too late; the convention business had already
moved on to the next item on the agenda. Where was the
Women's Political Caucus, the women's movement? There
should have been points of order raised, until at least the
offensive remarks were stricken from the convention record.
That is the minimum lesbians might have expected from
the women's movement, for which so many lesbians have
worked so hard for so long.

The trouble was, all of the minority groups were too busy
fighting their own battles to think of coalescing, and they
were too busy expressing hostility toward alien groups to
listen to the calls for help all around them. If all of the
oppressed groups at the convention had risen as one at the
first sign of oppression of *any of the other groups,* the convention would have had to stop and listen, and the oppressed
minorities would have been able to act as a patchwork but
effective majority. It did not happen at the convention. It
does not happen anywhere. It may never happen.

The women's movement must seriously try to shed itself
of its fears, hostility, and exploitation of lesbians as a group.
Only then can there be a true and workable connection between the feminist and the lesbian movements.

5

The Oppressor Church
... For the Bible Tells Me So

> *New York in 1965 adopted a new penal code replacing*
> *the code of 1909 as amended. "In its original form*
> *the code removed consensual sodomy and adultery*
> *from the list of criminal offenses. The code*
> *commissioners and legislative leaders, on the basis*
> *of their meetings with churchmen and other*
> *professional groups over a three year period, were*
> *confident of success. But as the time to vote drew*
> *near, the strong and open opposition of spokesmen*
> *for the Catholic Church, expressed in an eighteen-page*
> *memorandum sent to each legislator and in oral*
> *testimony at public hearings, caused legislators to get*
> *cold feet. By the vote of 115 to 16, the two contested*
> *acts were retained as criminal offenses.*
> —from The Challenge and Progress
> of Homosexual Law Reform, *testimony given by*
> *GAA, 1971 hearings on victimless crimes.*

> ARCHDIOCESE ASKS CITY COUNCIL TO
> DEFEAT BILL ON HOMOSEXUALS
> —*Headline,* The New York Times, *April 28, 1974*

The Catholic Church is a major oppressor of all women; it is a major deterrent of reform of archaic sex laws. These laws on "deviate sexual behavior" are often enforced against homosexuals, particularly politically active homosexuals,

56

but are usually unenforced against heterosexuals. They are church-state laws, and nothing to date has been done to work toward separation of church and state.

There is growing awareness among women in the feminist movement that the Church has been a key force in maintaining the laws responsible for the oppressed condition of women. Many of these same feminists, however, do not realize that *their own* attitudes about lesbianism have been created and reinforced by this same oppressor Church. They continue to promote the coin, in many instances, that homosexuality represents a "moral problem," never biting that coin to see if it is counterfeit. Although they have begun to question the mores which the Church has established in relation to women as a class, at the same time they often accept the church doctrine on homosexuality.

It is time to examine the hypocrisy of the Church in its oppression of those involved in victimless "crimes."

Gambling? Go to a Church fund-raising street fair: all events, save the food concessions, involve gambling. And don't forget the bingo.

Prostitution? Aside from the one out of three women in the United States whose marriages end in divorce, there are countless women who live out their lives in loveless marriages essentially because their husbands are "good providers." *The New York Times* of January 21, 1973, carried this item:

> Two members of the National Organization for Women spoke up for women's rights last week at the weekly luncheon meeting of the Yonkers Rotary Club. Much as its 15,306 fraternal counterparts around the world, the Yonkers club has no female members. The reaction to the speakers from NOW was a mixture of curiosity and animosity. Said Joseph Lennox, a retired but not

retiring admiral: "If my wife said anything about wom-
en's lib, I'd leave her. She's got a pocketful of credit
cards. What more freedom does she need?"

And yet the Church is adamant on the subject of prostitution.

Homosexuality? The Catholic Church oppresses the homosexual out of enlightened self-interest, the homosexual
being a non-procreator. Why else is the term "missionary
position" used to refer to the only sexual act which is not
frowned upon by the Church? The Church merely looks the
other way when married Catholic women and men together
commit what would otherwise be considered "deviate sexual behavior." A point which deserves closer scrutiny:

Monosexual communities—harems, the military, prisons,
girls' schools, boys' schools, the sports world of athletes—
give rise to a higher incidence of homosexual activities than
communities in which both sexes are present. In addition
to the natural homosexuals, some heterosexuals turn to an
alternative sexuality. The athletes of Ancient Greece were
known to have free and open sexual relationships with one
another. Today's athlete, if you look closely, also exhibits
homosexual behavior: when a good play has been made
in football, the men fall on one another, hugging and sometimes kissing; men fondly pat their teammates' behinds as
they go off into sportive battle. Such behavior would be
judged unseemly off the playing field—in, say, a business
office. But perhaps not in a monastery. Since in other all-
male communities homosexual acts take place, there can
be no doubt that homosexual acts take place between men
who go into the monosexual environment of the priesthood.

A Jesuit brother, Dr. Charles Wilson, who once spoke at
D.O.B., said that there is a high incidence of homosexuality
in religious orders. As a psychological counselor for his or-

der, he has found that one of the prevalent problems of the men is how to reconcile their natural homosexual feelings for each other with the prevailing antipathetic views of the church they are serving.

The "calling" which both priests and nuns are said to have has at no time been described as having a deadening effect on nerve endings, or on the natural sexual and emotional persuasions of the homosexual and homo-emotional men and women of the Church. There is no reason to assume that lesbian activities take place in other monosexual communities and not in the all-female society of the nunnery.

It is interesting to note that the accepted homosexual population figure does not include the high per capita incidence of homosexuality among members of the Church. The Church, by maintaining the charge of "sin against nature" against all homosexuals, continues to deny humanity and justice to those of its own numbers who are caught in the trap of judgmental attitudes which the Church has perpetuated throughout the centuries.

H. Montgomery Hyde, in his well-documented history of homosexuality, *The Love That Dared Not Speak Its Name* (Boston: Little, Brown & Company, 1970), notes:

> Unlike the people of Ancient Greece and the Arab countries in the Middle East, the Jews as depicted in the Old Testament strongly disapproved of homosexual conduct between males, and it was punishable by death. . . . No doubt the basis for its condemnation was similar to that of withdrawal in coitus, or Onanism . . . namely that it was the duty of the Jews to increase and multiply and any interference with the normal sexual function to this end was to be reprobated. "If a man also lie with mankind as he lieth with a woman, both of them have committed an abomination; they shall surely

be put to death; their blood shall be upon them." (Leviticus XX,13) Curiously enough no mention is made of female homosexuality in the Levitical law, nor for that matter anywhere else in the Bible with the exception of a single ambiguous passage in St. Paul's Epistle to the Romans (I, 26) proscribing women who "did change the natural use into that which is against nature." It has been suggested that this may mean no more than the reversal of the conventional coital position by which the woman lies underneath the man, and similar variations of methods which were practiced by Roman matrons, as we know from such pagan writers as Ovid and Apuleius. No doubt there were Hebrew women with lesbian habits in Biblical times just as there were in Ancient Greece, but they would not appear to have attracted the attention of the male lawgivers.

It would certainly appear from the celebrated account of the destruction of Sodom and Gomorrah in the nineteenth chapter of the Book of Genesis that the inhabitants of these "cities of the Plain" were given to homosexual practices, but they do not seem to have been more so than any of the other neighbouring Canaanite and Israelite towns and villages. . . . What then was the origin of the exclusively homosexual interpretation of the delinquencies of the Sodomites and their fellow citizens, which was later to have such a profound influence on the thinking and legislation of Christian communities on the subject? Incidentally, it is remarkable in this context that such scholarly sexologists as Havelock Ellis and Kinsey among others should have accepted the homosexual interpretation without question.

In addition to its clear position that homosexuality is patently inadmissible, the Catholic Church has another reason to oppress homosexuals: in order to maintain its status as a "moral leader." It must fight any change in attitude toward the church-state laws on homosexuality (or: abortion, divorce, prostitution, gambling) or it will lose its "moral" credibility. But the vigilance of the Church against sexual law reform must have another basis, as indeed it does: it is the carefully guarded tax-exempt status of the Church. In their book *Praise The Lord for Tax Exemption*, Dr. Martin A. Larson and the Reverend C. Stanley Lowell state:

> The Vatican business in the United States is only a small portion of that Church's wealth in this country. It might be noted in passing, however, that the Vatican may receive more than $1 billion annually in revenue from the Catholic parishes in the United States. We believe that lay Catholics would like to know precisely how much of their money flows in a golden stream to Rome; and that they would be amazed, should they learn the truth.
>
> The Roman Catholic Church is the largest religious organization in the United States. In common with other churches, it enjoys tax-exemption on its real estate and on both passive and active business income. Some idea of its real estate and other forms of wealth may be gathered from the remark of Thomas J. Gibbons, a lay official of the New York Catholic Conference, that this church probably ranks second only to the United States government in total annual purchases. A remarkable estimate of Catholic wealth was offered by the nationally syndicated priest, Fr. Richard Ginder, in the Diocesan paper, *Our Sunday Visitor:* "The Catholic Church must be the biggest corporation in the United States. We have a branch office in every neighborhood. Our assets and real estate holdings must exceed those of Standard Oil, A.T.&T. and U.S. Steel combined. And our roster of dues-paying members must be second only to the tax rolls of the United States Government."

In addition, the authors document among other things how the Church keeps its financial records secret from everybody, including its own members. The fact that the Church owns vast complexes of nonrelated businesses and income-producing properties of staggering worth (all of it virtually tax exempt) is a situation which has been challenged in a number of court cases. But the Church has constantly emerged from these battles in the "missionary position," that is, squarely on top.

The power of the Church, and its ever-expanding financial, ergo political, power is accepted by the masses of people in large part on the basis of the Church's being a moral leader; as a result, it will be a long, bleak time before sexual law reform will take place. The Church guards its dark-ages attitudes on sex as ferociously as it guards its wealth since, in the final analysis, the latter is dependent on the former.

Throughout history the Church has proclaimed homosexuality a "transgression against God." The Church has been instrumental for centuries in establishing that homosexuality, as a "sin," be punished as a "crime" in the legal sense. This can be historically outlined by excerpts from H. Montgomery Hyde's book:

> The conception of homosexual practices as the peculiar sin of Sodom was accepted by the early Christian Church and the word "sodomitical" in its Latin form came into use. . . . The precise treatment of homosexual offenders by the ecclesiastical authorities was set out in various manuals of penance for the use of confessors, known as The Penitentials, which originated in the Celtic Churches of Ireland and Wales and later spread to England and the European continent. . . . The subject was treated by St. Thomas Aquinas, who accepted the association with

Sodom and argued that, since what he called the *pecca-tum contra naturam* in any form was directed solely to the pursuit of venereal pleasure and *excluded procreation* [author's italics], it clearly offended against reason and consequently fell to be considered as one of the species of lust. . . . Early in the fourteenth century a homosexual, or more probably a bisexual, monarch mounted the English throne in the person of Edward II. . . . In 1327, when being held prisoner in Berkeley Castle, he was murdered after being tortured in a peculiarly revolting fashion at the instigation of his French consort Isabella and her lover Roger Mortimer. . . . The contemporary chronicler Ranulf Higden tells us that he was "sleyne with a hotte brooch putte thro the secret place posteriale," that is by the insertion of a burning stake in his anus. . . . Half a century later, in the reign of Edward II's son, Edward III, mention is made in parliamentary proceedings, apparently for the first time, of "the too horrible vice which is not to be named. . . ." This was in 1376 when the so-called Good Parliament unsuccessfully petitioned the king to banish all "Lombard brokers" alleging that they were usurers, and other foreign artisans and traders, particularly Jews and Saracens on the ground that they had introduced sodomitical practices which would destroy the realm. . . . By and large the charge of homosexuality seems to have been part of the general "smear" campaign employed by the Inquisition against its enemies. . . . The first detailed treatment of the subject "Of Buggery, or Sodomy," by a legal authority, apart from passing mention, occurs in the Third Part of Coke's *Institutes*. . . . On the history of the offence, the judge had this to say: "Our ancient Authors doe conclude, that it deserveth death, though they differ in the manner of the punishment. Britton saith, that Sodomites shall be burnt, and so were the Sodomites by Almighty God. Fleta saith, Sodomitae in terra vivi confodiantur (buried alive). But to say it

once for all the judgment in all cases of felony is that
the person attainted be hanged by the neck until he or
she be dead. But in ancient times in that case, the man
was hanged, and the woman was drowned. . . . The Act
of 25 Henry 8 hath adjudged it felony, and therefore
the judgment of felony doth now belong to this offence,
viz. to be hanged by the neck till he be dead. . . ." As
Coke suggests, the Preamble of the Act of 1533 is most
important in this context, since it clearly implies that
hitherto homosexual offences had been exclusively dealt
with by the ecclesiastical courts.

Male homosexuals were burned at the stake; the pejorative
term "faggot" is said to stem from this practice. Lesbians,
although on occasion punished, were usually excluded, or
rather, being "unimportant," they went virtually unnoticed.

These attitudes and practices passed from ecclesiastical
to secular authority and are the basis of the punitive legislation on the books today.

Church doctrine on homosexuality makes the oppression
of women by the Church especially virulent for the lesbian.
Open discussions at D.O.B. on lesbianism and the Church
made it clear that lesbian women were far more aware of
the Church's role in oppressing women than were their
heterosexual sisters.

An example: following Ti-Grace Atkinson's controversial
March 10, 1971, speech at Catholic University in Washington, D. C., during which she was physically attacked by
Mrs. Brent Bozell (sister of Senator James and columnist
William Buckley), D.O.B. was the only organization to
make any statement about the incident. Working with other
homophile groups, we organized a demonstration in front
of Saint Patrick's Cathedral in New York City on March

22, 1971. This is the leaflet which we prepared and passed out to the public and the press:

HOMOSEXUAL ORGANIZATIONS IN SUPPORT OF THE ATKINSON
STATEMENT ON CATHOLIC/POLITICAL OPPRESSION
OF WOMEN

Ti-Grace Atkinson's recent Catholic University speech on the oppression of women by the Catholic/Political complex made front page news from coast to coast.

It has since been conspicuously ignored by the Feminist Movement, other oppressed groups, editorial pages of newspapers and the Buckleys.

New York homophile organizations realize the political significance of the issue. Women and homosexuals are the major victims of the Catholic Church's oppression. Miss Atkinson, the only feminist with the courage to challenge the Church, was physically attacked by Mrs. Brent Bozell, wife of the editor of Triumph Magazine and sister of the "law and order" Buckleys.

We the undersigned are in unity with Miss Atkinson's indictment of the Catholic Church. It is a ruthless foe of abortion, sexual law reform, divorce, birth control and human dignity.

The Catholic Church (perhaps the most powerful financial corporation in the world) with its tax exempt status is a frightening contradiction of separation of church and state.

How much longer can conscientious citizens allow the Church to misuse its political power under the guise of religion?

Daughters of Bilitis New York
with members of:

Gay Activist Alliance
Gay Liberation Front
Gay Youth
Mattachine Society
New York University Gay Students' Liberation

Radical lesbians
Street Transvestite Action Revolutionaries

In the April D.O.B. Newsletter the following article appeared:

HOMOSEXUAL COMMUNITY SUPPORTS TI-GRACE ATKINSON
STATEMENT AT ST. PAT DEMONSTRATION

D.O.B. organized a press conference and demonstration at St. Patrick's Cathedral on Monday, March 22 at 11:30 A.M. in coalition with other New York Homophile organizations. The purpose was to show our community's support of the Ti-Grace Atkinson statement made recently at Catholic University in Washington, D.C.

Eight women from the D.O.B. Feminist Workshop accompanied Miss Atkinson to Washington, not as reported in the press to serve as her bodyguards, but rather to maintain security of the building in which she was to speak. This meant searching the building prior to the speech and performing searches of people attending the speech, as had been pre-arranged with the students at Catholic University. These plans were not carried out because of a questionable, last-hour Catholic University switch in the location of the speech and a take-over of the building by graduate student "marshals."

The day following the speech and the Buckley sister's attack on her, Miss Atkinson held a press conference (on this occasion Workshop women did secure the conference location and conducted searches of those attending). At this press conference Miss Atkinson made the first definitive statement on the political implication of Lesbianism to the feminist movement to be made by any feminist. This statement was also carried in papers around the nation with the notable exception of the *New York Times*. Miss Atkinson talked about her membership in D.O.B. and about the Feminist Workshop which she coordinates. She said further that the only women she trusted on the Catholic University trip were Lesbians.

Although many feminists were contacted prior to the St. Patrick's demonstration—some of whom said they would attend—only four feminists appeared, including Flo Kennedy * and Joan Hamilton.**

With the exception of these women, homosexuals made up the entire contingency, the first support—and the only public statement made to date—by any group, movement or individual woman.

Where is the feminist movement that not one "leader" or "follower" has come forward to support the first important attack on the taproot of women's oppression, the Church? Where are they, that the Atkinson statement went literally unnoticed, publicly, by them, although it made the front pages of newspapers across the country?

Homosexuals would like to know!

Although four television camera crews were on hand, along with reporters from Associated Press, United Press International and the New York *Daily News*, New York *Post* and the *Village Voice*, not one word about the demonstration appeared in any of the media.

Although not as powerful a political force as the Catholic Church (and therefore not as effective in halting law reform), the Protestant Church nevertheless upholds the attitude of homosexuality as a sin against nature and perpetuates the dissemination of misinformation to its congregations.

D.O.B., in its efforts to effect changes in attitudes and, hence, legislation, took the following action, as reported in the April 1971 Newsletter:

D.O.B. ACTION AT CENTRAL PRESBYTERIAN CHURCH

On Thursday evening, March 4, we turned our action meeting into an action!

We were told that the Central Presbyterian Church on

---

* Lawyer, feminist, author of *The Abortion Rap*.
** Activist in Black Liberation movement.

Park Avenue at 64th Street shows a weekly film and then holds a rap session about it in the church coffee shop. On March 4 the film was "The Fox."

We wanted to talk to the congregation about the unrealistic position and oppressiveness of the film. We wanted them to learn about our many other political oppressions. We also wanted to help our Gay Liberation Front sisters to liberate space at that church for dances.

At 9:30 P.M. we started assembling quietly in the church lobby. Some of us watched the film through a glass window while we waited. There were about a dozen of us.

We planned to wait until everyone was settled in the coffee shop and then walk in and confront them. It didn't work out that way. As the large crowd finally came out we saw them leaving the church.

Ruth Simpson acted quickly. She stopped the entire crowd and told them: "There is a group of Lesbians from Daughters of Bilitis and Gay Liberation Front here. You've just seen D. H. Lawrence's version of lesbianism. Why don't you join us to hear the Lesbian's version. Out of the closet and into the basement coffee shop."

The crowd changed direction and headed for the basement stairs. . . .

Soon the hostility ceased. Some people said that they hadn't realized how oppressed we were, but they didn't know how to change things.

In response to a statement from the moderator that churches were "beginning to understand the problem," Ruth said: "How do you expect us to believe you, since church doors have been closed to us one by one? If you are serious, let's discuss a specific: Will you rent the beautiful space here to a homosexual organization?"

This was met with silence.

Needless to say, the church did not rent the space to the women.

It should be pointed out that the congregation of this

68

particular church seemed to be "enlightened liberals." On the issue of homosexuality, however, they were totally uninformed or misinformed, and expressed bigoted, archaic views—none of which the church has ever tried to correct.

The intractability of the churches creates for the lesbian member a situation of hopelessness, guilt, and shame. At D.O.B. I met a number of women whose experience with their Catholic Church has caused them deep pain. Their backgrounds were often similar; many had "confessed" their lesbianism to their priests and had been met with crushing denunciations.

It is painfully interesting to note that while the middle-aged lesbian women who had raised their families and were in some instances past childbearing age were more or less ignored by their clergymen, the younger women—their child-bearing years still ahead of them—were frequently exposed to damaging verbal abuse.

When Ellen Povill was about twenty-eight years old, a Catholic friend of long standing told her that they could no longer be friends. She had admitted to her priest that she had a friend who was homosexual. He had admonished her to stop seeing Ellen, saying that she must have nothing whatsoever to do with her, that homosexuality is a dreadful sin, a crime against nature and God. Naturally upset, Ellen called Saint Patrick's Cathedral and asked to speak to a priest. She told him the story. The priest told Ellen that her friend was absolutely right to have told her priest, and that the priest had given her the only advice appropriate to save her from such a sinful association. Ellen attempted to discuss it further, but the priest hung up.

Partly on the basis of this experience, Ellen suggested that I research, on a direct one-to-one basis, the potency of the Church's oppression of lesbians. Her idea was that I would create a fictional background, go to Saint Patrick's Cathedral, ask to see a priest, and see what response I got when I told him my "problem." This is the history I developed for the woman I would claim to be: I was Mrs. Marie Cutrone, forty-six years old, married for twenty-six years, the mother of three children, Anthony (twenty-five), Josephine (twenty-three), and Aida (nineteen). All of my children lived away from home. I had been away from the Church for quite a while. My husband and I had lost interest in each other, both emotionally and sexually, a number of years ago. Since the children were grown I was allowed to get a job a little more than three years ago. There was a woman who worked with me to whom I had developed a very strong attraction. I desperately needed help. (Actually, this was a conglomerate history of a number of women I had met in the movement.)

On January 2, 1973, I went to Saint Patrick's, to find the cathedral filled with a large and intricate scaffolding. In addition to the many collection boxes for "The Poor of the World" there were other boxes marked "For the Renovation of Saint Patrick's Cathedral." There was no priest in the church, but I did find a custodian who was collecting baskets. I asked him if I could see a priest and he directed me to the Rectory. A short while later a young priest approached and led me into his office. I unfolded my "history." He immediately got up and closed the door.

FATHER GENET: How long have you been married?

MARIE: Twenty-six years.

FATHER GENET: Oh, twenty-six years, yes, well sometimes after a long time people do have this problem.

MARIE: I have been so upset that I went to the library

70

to see what I could find on the subject of homosexuality, but most information is on males. I couldn't find anything on lesbianism.

FATHER GENET: (visibly agitated) But you aren't a lesbian. You still have your husband. You must be *watchful*. You must be watchful, because you know what problems you would create. Have you and this woman . . . have you gone beyond the boundaries . . . have you . . . I mean there is nothing wrong with your having a friendship, but you must be watchful. Have you gone beyond the boundaries?

MARIE: We have not had any physical relationship, but the attraction is very strong.

FATHER GENET: Have you talked about this to your husband?

MARIE: I couldn't possibly tell him about my feelings for my friend, he would have fits, and . . .

FATHER GENET: Oh, of course, you could not discuss that with him, but have you talked to him about your marriage?

MARIE: Many times. I have tried, but he doesn't think there is anything wrong with the marriage.

FATHER GENET: Do you sleep together?

MARIE: We have twin beds. But it isn't only that he has lost interest in me sexually. It's that we have nothing to share any more and when I tried to talk about our marriage, which I stopped trying some time ago, he was always flip, or he would get mad.

FATHER GENET: What sort of thing would he say? Has he ever—

MARIE: Oh, he's never been physically mean, but we don't communicate. I feel that my life would be over if it were not for the feeling I have for my friend.

71

FATHER GENET: Yes, but you must be watchful. How often do you see this woman? Do you see her outside of work?

MARIE: Once in a while we have dinner together, when I know my husband isn't coming home.

At this point he asked me about my relationship with my children and asked if I had discussed this with Josephine, my married daughter. I replied that I couldn't possibly discuss my friend and my feelings for her with my children.

FATHER GENET: Of course not, but have you discussed your marital problems with her?

MARIE: No, I feel that isn't her problem. There is no one for me to talk to about it and my husband doesn't even know I came here today.

FATHER GENET: Well, as I've said, you must be watchful, because you know the problems involved if you should go beyond the boundaries. You would create problems for everybody.

MARIE: Yes, but I need help. I can't find any books on the subject of homosexuality that give any helpful information on lesbianism. I need some professional guidance.

FATHER GENET: (turning from his desk and reaching for a book) Well, perhaps you would like to call our Counseling Service. Yes, perhaps you should call there and they might be able to help you. You can call and set up an appointment. You can say that I suggested that you call.

Father Genet wrote out a number, an address, and his name. I stood up to leave. As we got to the door he turned and said, "You must be watchful, because you know if this goes beyond the boundaries it could cause little problems around the house." Marie, not quite sure what that meant, said, "Yes, Father, and thank you."

By this time my knees were a little shaky. It had taken some steeling of the nerves to carry this through and to field some of the unexpected questions. But the nervousness had served me well, because I was able to incorporate it as part of Marie's nervousness. I was aware of the persistence I had to bring to bear on Father Genet in order to convince him that my feelings for a woman were a real problem. A problem which embarrassed admonitions about being "watchful" and vague talk of "boundaries" were not going to solve. I wondered how many women have not been able, because of guilt, to press enough to receive even a promise of help. What form that "help" might take was still to be seen.

I went home and dialed the number Father Genet had given me. The woman who answered set up an appointment for me with a Father Carroll, for the following Tuesday, January 9. She asked for a telephone number in case the appointment had to be changed.

MARIE: Oh, I can't give you my home phone because my husband must not know about this.

WOMAN: I understand, but could you leave your office number and we will be very careful if we have to call. I'll just say that Diane is calling.

I gave her Ellen's office number. I then said that if I were recommended to a psychiatrist, how much would that be, because money would be a problem. She said that it would go according to income, and that it might run around $15.00. In the meantime, I should come in and talk to Father Carroll.

73

On January 9 I arrived at the Archdiocese and was directed to the Counseling Service. There I was given an extensive form to fill out which asked family history, work association, income, and education. Shortly after, I was ushered into Father Carroll's office. It was a nervous Marie Cutrone who faced the intense, attractive, bearded priest.

FATHER CARROLL: Won't you sit down. What brings you here?

Marie retold her story.

FATHER CARROLL: Yes, well, have you talked to your husband about your problem?
MARIE: Oh, I couldn't possibly discuss this with him.
FATHER CARROLL: But can't you discuss your marriage with him?
MARIE: I tried in the beginning. Until I met my friend I had nothing, and now I don't know what to do.

At this point Father Carroll asked questions about Marie's relationships with her daughters, her son, and her parents.

FATHER CARROLL: Well, I think it would be a good idea if you could come in with your husband.
MARIE: Oh, I couldn't possibly talk about this in front of him. That would be impossible.
FATHER CARROLL: You mean that you can't discuss your marriage with your husband?
MARIE: Yes, I suppose so, but that is only a part of the problem. This friend of mine—I can't tell you how important she has become in my life.
FATHER CARROLL: Well, it would be a good idea if you and your husband could come in. It is customary to dis-

cuss problems with both parties of the couple. Let's see, your husband drives a truck. What time could he come in?

MARIE: He has to return his truck to the yard in Brooklyn.

FATHER CARROLL: Yes, time might be a problem, but could he get here by, say, ten after five?

MARIE: He couldn't possibly make it before at the very earliest close to five-thirty. But, Father, he doesn't even know I am here and I didn't tell him about my talk with Father Genet. And I couldn't talk about what may be the major part of my problem. I mean there were a couple of times, oh, years ago, when I felt attracted to women friends, but nothing like this.

FATHER CARROLL: Well, if you can bring your husband in, perhaps we can work out some of the problems of your marriage, or if you decide that you can't work them out, you might make the decision to make it on your own.

MARIE: Do you think I should try to talk about the entire problem with my husband?

FATHER CARROLL: Don't you think it would be best to see if you can't work out some of the problems of your marriage? Then, if you can't, you can make the decision as to whether you might want to make it on your own.

MARIE: I have tried to find out about homosexuality from books in the library, but there doesn't seem to be much on females. I feel that I need some sort of professional help with this.

FATHER CARROLL: When is the last time you tried to discuss your marriage with your husband? Has it been recently?

MARIE: Oh, I gave up trying to do that. So often it would end up in an argument.

FATHER CARROLL: Well, you will have to decide what you

want to do, whether you want to come back with your husband, or if you want to come back without your husband and discuss it further.

MARIE: I guess I'll have to think it over. It probably would be best if I talked to my husband about coming here, but I don't think he's going to like it. And, besides, I can't discuss the entire problem with him.

FATHER CARROLL: Well, why don't you think about it and then call back. We can make an appointment then if you would like.

MARIE: All right, I guess this will take some real mind-joggling on my part. Thank you, Father, and I will call back, no matter what I decide.

I left Father Carroll's office and was walking through the reception room when one of the women at the desk said, "Oh, Mrs. Cutrone, that will be ten dollars."

I was really embarrassed for poor Marie, who said, "Oh, I didn't know that there would be a charge. I don't have money, except some change with me. Would it be all right if I sent it to you? Or I will probably be coming back. If I do, I can bring it and pay for everything then." (I could hardly have written a check.)

The young woman said that it was perfectly all right—I could either mail it or bring it on my next visit.

I left the Archdiocese and walked some twenty blocks home. Very carefully I went over the interview in my memory to make sure that I kept it vivid and clear. I think that I have left nothing important out and I believe I have set it down as accurately as possible. I think that I have not done Father Carroll any disservice; I believe I have quoted him correctly. The interview went basically, if not verbatim, the way I have recorded it here.

At no time during the long interview did the religious, male authority-figure ask one question about Marie's friend; at no point did he acknowledge Marie's statements about her attraction to another woman or her questions about her sexuality. He ignored the entire situation and addressed himself only to how it might be possible to salvage her marriage. The only oblique—and it was so oblique as to be almost nonexistent—reference to any problem other than her marriage was his "make it on your own" alternative to her failing marriage. To a woman in Marie's position (and I have known several), such an alternative, without even the consideration of the possibility of perhaps some sort of relationship with her friend, would be totally threatening. The priest, without having even discussed the woman's friend or her feelings for her friend, certainly did not design the alternative of "making it on your own" to bolster her sense of self or her state of well-being.

I discussed the interview with a very few close friends in the lesbian and feminist movements and it was agreed that the poor Maries of the world would at this point be confused, solitary, and defeated. There is much credit due to such women who have the strength to make it to D.O.B. I often wonder what becomes of the Maries who do not.

The question arises: Would all churches have dealt with a woman like Marie in the same way? There is no practical method of finding out. But from observation of hundreds of lesbians I have known, it is clear that many lesbian women have either developed a degraded self-image because of the attitudes of their churches, or they have recognized, because of attitudes expressed by the clergy, that their churches are their oppressors. The Bible tells them so.

6

Lesbianism and Psychiatry
Either Conform or Maladjust

The September 25, 1970, issue of Medical World News, *a respected professional journal, heralded a method of "treating" the homosexual: Dr. Fritz Roeder, a psychosurgeon, concentrates on the "patient's" hypothalamus gland (a section of the forebrain). He "treats" it by burning it out electrically.*

The American Psychiatric Association, altering a position it has held for almost a century, decided today that homosexuality is not a mental disease. The Board of trustees voted instead to categorize homosexuality as a "sexual orientation disturbance" rather than a "mental disorder."
—The New York Times, *December 16, 1973*

What you have in a homosexual adult is a person whose heterosexual function is crippled like the legs of a polio victim. . . . Are you going to say that this is normal?
—*Dr. Irving Bieber, quoted in*
The New York Times, *December 23, 1973*

The great majority of those in the psychiatric and psychology fields regard homosexuality as, at best, a gross maladjustment and recommend various "cures" for it. The fact is, the general attitude of the profession is based in the Church's "crime against nature" dictum. This is expressed succinctly in the

78

following quotation from psychiatrist Frank Caprio's *Female Homosexuality:*

> An American correspondent, in one of Havelock Ellis' volumes of *Sex Studies,* wrote: "I believe that sexual inversion is increasing among Americans—both men and women—and the obvious reasons are: first the growing independence of the women. . . . In a word the rapidly increasing *masculinity in women* and the unhealthy nervous system of the men offer the ideal factor for the production of sexual inversion in their children." [Author's note: He does not explain how this could possibly work biologically or in any other way.]
>
> There are many today who would be willing to support the above contention, convinced that this new freedom which women are enjoying serves as fertile soil for the seeds of sexual inversion. It is not too surprising in the face of all the changes that are taking place in our modern society [i.e., the Feminist Movement] that many frustrated, pleasure seeking unmarried women prefer to replace heterosexuality with an exploitation of sexuality amongst themselves which is contrary to a woman's basic needs. Women unconsciously prefer to fulfill their maternal role and to be loved by a man. As Dr. [Bernard] Bauer so aptly expressed it: "Fredom for women means freedom to love. But we cannot go against Nature. Woman is intended for reproduction; she has been appointed to take an active part in the reproduction of the race by pregnancy and child-birth. And while these laws of Nature remain every attempt at emancipation is futile."

Dr. Caprio goes on to say, "Psychoanalysts are in agreement that all women who prefer a homosexual way of life suffer from a distorted sense of values and betray their emotional immaturity in their attitude towards men, sex and marriage."

Any woman's hackles ought to rise on reading Dr. Bauer's

79

statement. And yet many "feminists" blindly accept the Church's, and the psychiatric profession's, indoctrination, on lesbianism. To these women, homosexuality is "sick"— or worse. To take one example: Germaine Greer appeared on the Public Broadcasting Service on February 12, 1973, in the program, "Cambridge Debate." In speaking about her detractors, Miss Greer said, "And, of course, I have been awarded the booby prize of being labeled a lesbian or a maniac." She went on to assure her audience that she as a feminist is not a "sexual deviant."

Miss Greer is certainly familiar with the psychiatric profession's oppression of women, and speaks out against it . . . except when that oppression happens to be directed against the ten per cent or more of all women who are lesbians.

As evidence of the widespread agreement of psychiatrists that "Lesbians are women who won't conform to the laws of Nature," statements and papers from seventeen psychiatrists were collected into one volume. The credentials of these sixteen men and one woman are too numerous to list here, but they are indeed impressive. The major part of the book deals with homosexuality, but this subject, as is so often the case, is lumped together with sado-masochism, male genital exhibitionism, and fetishism. And the name of the book tells the whole story. It is *Perversions—Psychodynamics and Therapy*, edited by Sandor Lorand and Michael Balint (London: Ortolan Press, 1965).

From one contributor, Sandor S. Feldman: "It is the consensus of many contemporary psychoanalytic workers that permanent homosexuals, like all perverts, are neurotics. . . . Let us not forget that there is rarely a neurosis without some perversion and rarely a perversion without some neurotic symptoms." From Dr. Gustav Bychowski:

The latent homosexual constellation is a constant and most significant element of latent schizophrenia. This constellation centers around a primitive maternal identification which, by virtue of splitting, remains isolated from the rest of the ego field. . . . The personality structure of drug addicts shows, in many instances, elements of latent or manifest homosexuality. . . . This point of view also makes clear the dynamic reasons for the frequent combination of addiction and certain forms of criminality. . . . In my observations of neurotic obesity, I become aware of the role played by repressed homosexuality in my predominantly female patients. . . . Finally, we have to consider the role of homosexuality in that most popular and best-known addiction, alcoholism. . . . I can confirm that women with a strong homosexual component resort to drinking as a means of identifying and competing with men.

In my years in the homosexual movement I have met many fewer alcoholics than in my years in the Madison Avenue public relations field; "neurotic obesity" is not, despite the implication of the doctor, a corollary or side-effect of homosexuality. One need only note the basically heterosexual women who frequent the Elizabeth Arden–type figure salons; and Weight Watchers is hardly a haven for homosexual women. Drug addiction is a social phenomenon which has attacked our culture across the board. Addiction is a social problem which cannot logically be relegated to the homosexual population.

That same book contains many more doctors' theories and case histories and methods of "cure." Ironically, the psychiatrists who have appointed themselves the "experts" on homosexuality have done the most damage to both homosexuals and heterosexuals by way of dictating "scientific" negative attitudes and cures which have been accepted as viable, but which in fact have done tremendous sociolog-

81

ical and emotional damage. These "experts" are, notably, the Drs. Socarides, Caprio, Bergler, Hatterer, Kaye and Bieber. These are the "authorities" quoted most frequently on the subject of "treatment and cure of the homosexual."

Of the group, Dr. Socarides is particularly virulent, since he has written so voluminously and, so often, addressed himself to other doctors, "instructing" them on how to "treat" homosexuals. He appears in the media as an authority and presents his incredibly narrow, self-conceived theories which have nothing whatsoever to do with the millions of homosexuals in the country, whether these homosexuals function from within or without the confines of closets.

I would like to deal specifically with an article by Dr. Socarides that appeared in the *Journal of the American Medical Association,* May 18, 1970, Vol. 212, No. 7, pages 1199–1202. I do not include the notes, which appear at the end of the article, but it should be pointed out that of the eighteen reference sources, ten are taken from Dr. Socarides' own writings.

Since Dr. Socarides touches on so many points and promulgates so many current misconceptions I have found it useful to add my comments and rebuttals immediately after each allegation in this "static debate."

HOMOSEXUALITY AND MEDICINE
Charles W. Socarides, M.D.
The issue of homosexuality is dominated by emotional thinking which can not help but generate confusion, fear, and rage.

Indeed, there is confusion and fear surrounding the issue of homosexuality, since there has been little or no information until recently on the subject other than that developed by heterosexuals who "diagnose," "treat," and ultimately condemn homosexuals for nonconformity. To draw a comparison, it is only recently that black history has begun to be taught, that black identity has begun to emerge. Whites have been spelling out what blacks need, want, deserve or don't deserve. By the same token, heterosexuals are spelling out what it means to be homosexual via the institutions of this country which are white, male, and heterosexual in structure and outlook. As to the "rage" the good doctor mentions, it does indeed exist, in two forms: the rage of the homosexuals who will no longer accept Socarides' evaluation of us, and the rage of the heterosexuals who have learned to hate us through this evaluation.

> These charged attitudes, at first individual, have become widespread throughout the community and compound the difficulties in dealing with this major health problem.

In my extensive dealings with homosexuals, I have observed no more "health problems" among homosexuals, per capita, than I have observed among my heterosexual friends.

> Homosexuality, overt but also covert, upsets us.

Who is "us"? Not most homosexuals . . . only those whom your "they are sick" theories have upset. And of course you have upset a great many heterosexuals who, since you are an "authority," accept your appraisal of us.

> Polls have shown that the majority of the public still favors legal punishment for homosexual acts even if performed in private.

Polls will continue to show this until accurate information on homosexuality is made available to the public.

> . . . homosexuality is considered more harmful to society

83

> than adultery and even than abortion with its actual
> threat to life.

"Abortion," with "its actual threat to life"? Your umbilical cord to the church is still attached.

> In our culture the very thought of effeminacy in the
> male is tremendously disturbing.

Yes, in our culture the brutal national sport of football, for instance, is a criterion of normalcy. Two men in love, or who just like each other a lot, walk down the street holding hands, and you label them "sick." But let two teams of men batter each other in sportive battle, and, lo, you have the American ideal of manhood.

> The historical evidence of the practice of homosexuality from earliest recorded times has led to grave misconceptions. One can often discern in the homosexual a feeling that if this condition has been extant over so many centuries what hope is there for him. Surely his fate is sealed. This defeatism infiltrates the public and unfortunately influences our laws and our scientific objectivity.

We do not feel defeated, despite your efforts. Your "scientific objectivity" is highly suspect, since you base your efforts on *our*, homosexual, defeatism. In other words, your premise is merely another statement of your conclusion, so that anyone who doubts the truth of your conclusion surely ought to be equally doubtful about the truth of your premise.

> Rather than assume that homosexuality, like poverty, is
> an inevitable component of the human condition . . .

You have really given up on poverty? You *accept* that in this heterosexual, male-dominated world, poverty should go unchallenged, untreated as a cultural illness?

84

> . . . it better behooves us to acknowledge that homosex-
> uality is a form of mental illness which has not yet been
> adequately studied by those who are best trained to in-
> vestigate and treat it.

If homosexuality were allowed to be investigated by those
who are best trained to investigate it, namely, functioning
homosexuals, it would soon become evident that it is not a
mental illness. As for treatment, only those homosexuals
who have been damaged by the degraded self-image which
is promoted would need to be helped along the road to hu-
man-hood.

> Reports on the therapeutic outcome have changed the
> clinical prognosis from an essentially pessimistic one to
> one in which at least one third of life-long, exclusively
> homosexual patients can become exclusively heterosex-
> ual.

Therapy in terms of a "cure" is, in the first place, unacceptable to us. You must know that to remove the option of
identity from a human being is at the same time to remove humanity from that human being. I know of many
women who were assured by your profession that they were
"cured" but found, one husband and several children later,
that they were incapable of continuing in a life that to them
was unnatural. Their re-entry into their natural climate of
homosexuality then had not only the burdens of our society
but the additional burdens of a husband and one or more
children, all innocent victims of your "miracle cures."

> Attempts to obfuscate the fact that homosexuality is a
> medical problem have not been met head on by those
> most qualified to clarify the situation. . . . Only in the
> consultation room does the homosexual reveal himself
> and his world. No other data, statistics or statements can
> be accepted as setting forth the true nature.

Since the first Christopher Street Gay Pride March, on June 28, 1970, involved approximately ten thousand homosexuals, it appears your consultation room would have proved a trifle small. Since the first Gay Pride March, there have been others—the 1974 Gay Pride marchers numbered around forty-three thousand (one of the largest groups ever to walk New York City streets). We would have overflowed the consultation rooms of the entire psychiatric profession.

> All other sources may be heavily weighted by face-saving devices or rationalizations or, if they issue from lay bodies, lack the scientific and medical background to support their views. The best that can be said for the well-intentioned but unqualified observer is that he is misguided because he does not have and can not apply those techniques which would make it possible to discern the deep, underlying clinical disorder or to evaluate the emotional patterns and interpersonal events in the life of a homosexual.

In other words, anyone who disagrees with you is "unqualified." What of those few in your own profession who do not regard homosexuals as sick?

> There are many doctors who by ignoring and disregarding homosexuality hope to render it invisible or nonexistent. To acknowledge it would be tantamount, they fear, to permitting it. In my opinion, part of medicine's neglect has been due not only to uncertainty concerning etiology, treatment, and prognosis but also that acceptance of homosexuality as a medical disorder alongside all other medical disorders has been unconsciously and consciously perceived by us as tantamount to being in favor of it, encouraging it, and perhaps endorsing it, thereby putting us in direct conflict with established standards of human conduct. This, I have discovered, is the current status of the problem of homosexuality on the part of many colleagues in the medical profession in

86

respect to a dread dysfunction, malignant in character, which has risen to epidemiologic proportions.

What an indictment the doctor levels at his own profession. If, indeed, homosexuality were the "dread dysfunction, malignant in character" which it has been labeled, are these professionals so unstable as to believe that acknowledging homosexuality would be tantamount to "encouraging," "endorsing," and being "in favor" of it? How unscientific! What renders this "illness" any different from tuberculosis or cancer, the common cold, or faulty nutrition?

> Exact statistics on homosexual practices are understandably difficult to compile; a conservative estimate is that between 2,500,000 and 4 million adult American males suffer from this condition.

The figure is at least 20 million. True, your false statistics cover only the male population: did you forget that there are also women in this country?

> By way of comparison a Public Health Service report estimated the four major illnesses in this country (1963–65) as: heart disease, 3,619,000; arthritis and rheumatism, 3,481,000; impairment (except paralysis) of the back and spine, 1,769,000; mental and nervous disease, 1,767,000.

If you really believe your "findings" on homosexuality and update the statistic on the homosexual population, then, your last figure there should read: mental and nervous disease, 21,767,000.

> The female homosexual finds herself in a paradoxical situation. Although suffering in essence with the same disorder as her male counterpart, little concern has been manifest by either the legal or medical professions about her condition. She too, however, needs special medical, legal and sociological consideration.

The position of the female homosexual is not much more paradoxical than the female position in general is. We both are "privileged" by having little concern manifested by the institutions in behalf of our condition. You are wrong, however, about our not receiving legal consideration. As soon as lesbians *organize* they are no longer "just women"; suddenly they become extra-legal women, and I, as president of D.O.B., appeared in court five times as evidence of this fact.

> Many writers prefer to use the term "lesbianism" to describe the clinical condition of female homosexuals. This reflects an attempt to romanticize and minimize it. Homosexual relations between women are often considered superficial, and some sources do not regard female homosexual contacts as sexual at all despite intense orgastic experiences between the women involved. Nevertheless, their plight is as grave if not more so than that of the male homosexual. For example, the loss of a homosexual partner can lead the bereft female homosexual to severe depressions and suicide with greater frequency than in the male.

Writers who described Lesbos and Sappho's followers were writing centuries before we were born, and were not considering "clinical conditions." Nor were they concerned with romanticizing or minimizing lesbianism. There are words which will remain in the language, no matter how you might try to wish them away. Yes, homosexual relations between women *are* often considered superficial, since woman's role in this and other cultures receives minimal attention of the established institutions. As to your vague reference to "some sources" which "do not regard female homosexual contacts as sexual at all," your logic eludes me since you follow that statement with "despite intense orgastic experiences between the women involved." Since when is orgasm a nonsexual phenomenon? I don't know whom your "sources" have been talking to, but obviously not to healthy lesbians who have natural sexual relationships. And to my knowledge there is no information that the percentage of suicides in the lesbian community is any higher than in the heterosexual or male homosexual community.

> I have dealt intensively with the illnesses diagnosed as perversion, especially with homosexuality, for the past 15 years—both in clinical practice and in teaching. Our first step is to ask ourselves "What is a homosexual?"

It would seem more logical not to ask *yourselves* "What is a homosexual?" but rather to ask that question of a homosexual. You are much more likely to get an accurate answer. Would you ask a homosexual, "What is a heterosexual?" Undoubtedly not.

> In essence, a homosexual is a person who consistently and from inner necessity engages in homosexual acts.

Here we go with the "pear tree is a tree that grows pears" theory. "A heterosexual, in essence, is a person who consistently and from inner necessity engages in heterosexual acts." The problem here is, you didn't answer your question at all; you simply made a circular statement.

> This pattern arises from faulty sexual identity, a product of the earliest years of life. Typically we find a pathological family constellation in which there is a domineering, crushing mother who will not allow the developing child to achieve autonomy from her and an absent, weak, or rejecting father.

The fifteen years you have spent in clinical and teaching practice, from what you say, have been spent in urging faulty sexual identity on homosexuals. As for your "family constellation" pathology, some of your own colleagues agree

89

that the "familial case histories" of homosexuals are as varied as those of heterosexuals. And remember that in many instances two children of identical backgrounds grow up to be, one a heterosexual and the other a homosexual.

> There are two categories of homosexuality: obligatory (true) homosexual and episodic homosexual behavior. The latter is characterized by isolated homosexual acts without the stereotypy, the compulsivity, of the former and is due to the conscious desire for variational experience, the achievement of "special gains," such as power and prestige, or the quest of unusual sensations.

Probably one could, if one wished to, similarly categorize heterosexuals as "obligatory" (the kind who just go at it all the time), and "episodic" (perhaps the man who seldom has sexual relations with his wife but makes occasional visits to prostitutes—I believe your profession has developed a designation for this: "the Madonna/Prostitute Syndrome"). But what would be the point? You create further confusion, however; since you regard homosexuality as a great sickness, what prestige of power, in your mind, is achieved by the episodic homosexual? Given your theories, this seems a gross contradiction.

> Such transient behavior may occur in specific situations as well; it may be rampant in prisons, remote settlements, or during other types of confinement where persons of the opposite sex are not available.

Such as in cloistered religious orders, the military, and the sports world.

> Except for those already predisposed to homosexuality through early psychological trauma the individual reverts to heterosexual behavior when members of the opposite sex are again available.

90

We know of a number of instances where both women and men have experienced homosexual relationships under conditions such as you describe and did not "revert" because they found that homosexuality was actually their natural orientation.

> There is a high incidence of paranoia or paranoid-like symptomatology in overt homosexuals.

When oppressed people react to their oppression, this isn't paranoia—it's for real. Acknowledgment of one's sociological condition can hardly be called paranoia, unless, of course, one wishes to obfuscate the oppression which creates that sociological condition.

> This is related to the medical fact that overt obligatory homosexuality is either a fixation or regression to the earliest stages of ego development.

Again, your circular reasoning: it is true because I say it is true. You and the medical profession, hand-in-hand with religious and other institutions, call homosexuality sick or sinful and then, when homosexuals respond negatively, you call them paranoid. Then you explain away their "paranoia" by calling it regression to the earliest stages of ego development. Actually, you keep regressing into your own self-devised terminology and theories, which have as much bearing on homosexuals as does Freud's penis-envy theory on the millions of women around the world who are striving toward full citizenship.

> As a result, archaic and primitive mental mechanisms belonging to the earliest stages of life characterize the homosexual's behavior. Also, homosexuals, obligatory or not, can be seen in the schizophrenic in his frantic attempt to establish some vestige of object relations as an

expression of the fragmented and disorganized psychic apparatus with which he has to struggle.

How's that again?

It is misleading to classify homosexuality as a sociopathic disorder.

We finally agree on something.

Not all homosexuals, or perhaps even a majority, display the "absence of conscience" mechanism so characteristic of the so-called psychopath.

The "absence of conscience" mechanism is overtly manifest in this and other governments which consistently engage in immoral wars and inhumane oppression of masses of people. Don't lay the "so-called psychopath" label on us, doctor. There are too many others, mostly heterosexual males, who deserve it far more.

The compulsivity of the sexual expression, its insistence for expression despite all dangers to the contrary and all risks, gives the appearance that one does not care about established social institutions or about oneself. The annals of political history include personalities at the very highest levels, men with an exceptionally well-developed sense of public and social good who have experienced the tragic consequences of their homosexual illness.

Wait until the first Homosexual History Week is instituted —a lot of people will be surprised at the roster. Again, homosexuality is not an illness, as an ever-increasing number of your colleagues today attest. Dr. Wardell B. Pomeroy, New York psychologist, says: "I've seen many homosexuals who were happy, who were participating and conscientious members of the community. . . . To insist they are abnormal, sick, or neurotic just because they're homosexual is to engage in circular reasoning which smacks of blind moralism." "Homosexuality is a way of loving, not a pathology," according to Lawrence LeShan, a well-known psychologist. Dr. Ruth Benedict, an eminent anthropologist, says: "Any neuroses or abnormal behavior can be attributed to the [homosexuals'] burden of guilt which society places on them."

> I ask you when you take a sexual history to respond with interest and compassion to efforts on the patient's part to communicate his shame and despair in the guilty revelation of behavior so demeaning and injurious to pride. At this point we must make certain definitive statements gained from our clinical research and accumulated knowledge of the human psyche in health and in illness: The claim that homosexuality is simply a variant of normal sexual behavior and exists alongside heterosexuality as an equivalent expression of adult sexual maturation is utterly false:

This is the "circular reasoning" of which both I and Dr. Pomeroy spoke. You have set yourself up as the housemother of morality.

> 1. True obligatory homosexuality is a form of psychiatric or emotional illness. After detailed exploration the Committee on Public Health of the New York Academy of Medicine reported its finding that homosexuality is a mental disorder whose only effective treatment is psychotherapy. The committee, totaling 30 members, consisted of several deans of medical schools, prominent representatives of medical specialties including six psychiatrists, the then commissioner of police of the city of New York as well as members of the judiciary. This 1964 report recognized homosexuality as an illness of social proportions, national significance, and serious portent.

You had better believe that we are serious. The credentials of the Committee are impressive, by *your* standards. After all you are considered a "prominent representative" of your field. We are not impressed. And as for the "then commissioner of police of the city of New York," you really cannot be serious. The police in this and other cities (and this is known by any serious person in any movement) will beat the heads of any group which is pointed out to them by the establishment as needing "attention." The Wolfenden Report was put together in England by an equally impressive committee, which, as you know, decided that we are legal.

> 2. Homosexual object choice is not innate or instinctual, nor is heterosexual object choice, since both are learned behavior. The choice of sexual object is not predetermined by chromosomal tagging. Heterosexual object choice is determined from birth due to cultural and environmental indoctrination.

Another contradiction. You say on one hand that heterosexual object choice is "learned behavior." How then can it be "determined from birth"? It can't be both ways.

> It is supported by universal human concepts of mating . . .

Not "universal," doctor; it is supported by *heterosexual* human concepts.

> . . . and the family unit with the complimentariness and contrast between the two sexes.

This may be true for many heterosexuals, although today some of these values are under question by heterosexuals themselves. But this pretty set of values simply does not apply to the homosexual community.

94

It is further determined by 2½ billion years of human evolution . . .

During all this time there has also been homosexuality, to greater or lesser degrees, depending on the culture or society. There is simply no way to ignore this fact—unless you choose to.

> . . . and is a product of sexual differentiation, at first solely based on reproduction but later widened to include sexual gratification, e.g., from one-celled non-sexual fission the development of two-celled sexual reproduction to separate entire organ differentiation and finally to the development of separate individuals reciprocally adapted to each other anatomically, endocrinologically, psychologically, and in many other ways.
> 3. Homosexual behavior which is nonobligatory (episodic) is practiced by individuals through choice for a variety of motivations and should not be confused with true homosexuality. These motivations are as complex as any other motivations which may influence human behavior: personal gain, power, search for variational experience (an extra sexual "thrill"), preferred status and position, etc. This form is not caused by unconscious fears and ensuing guilt but is due to conscious deliberate choice. One must carefully differentiate between the obligatory and the nonobligatory, as the latter type would like to mask behind true homosexuality in order to save pride and justify its occurrence.

It appears, from what you say, that the "motivations" of your nonobligatory homosexual, i.e., personal gain, power, status and position, are similar to those which may influence all human behavior. They don't seem to upset you as motivations in and for themselves. To me they seem self-serving and unattractive. But it is such motives which "save" the nonobligatory homosexual from your dread illness

95

which as you contend is accompanied by "behavior so demeaning and injurious to pride." "True" homosexuality, to use your term, seems to have the potential for better character development than your "episodic" homosexual. You talk about the episodic homosexual's attempt to "save pride" by masking behind true homosexuality. What is it you're saying—that we do or do not have pride?

> 4. Since the obligatory homosexual is suffering from an illness, it is obvious that he should not be penalized for the consequent activities carried out in private, not offensive to public decency, and in partnership with a consenting adult. He should not be made to suffer special penalties because of the manifestation of his illness, so long as it is not accompanied by antisocial or criminal behavior. The view that obligatory homosexuality per se is punishable by law and the view that it is, in fact, a medical problem are antithetical and this matter requires revision. However, any change in the legal code should be accompanied by a clarifying statement as to the nature of obligatory homosexuality, its diagnosis as a form of mental illness, and a universal declaration of support for its treatment by qualified medical practitioners.

Now, there's the clinker. It's like saying, yes, let's revise the laws which discriminate against blacks, but let's accompany those revised laws with a "universal declaration" which will clarify the fact that blacks are "lazy," "inferior," etc. Thanks, doctor!

> The Wolfenden report succeeded in having legislation passed in England redressing the inequities faced by the homosexual, but it regrettably failed both the homosexual and the public by not making it explicit that homosexuality is an emotional illness and, therefore, lies within the province of medicine. One might have recommended this addition to the Wolfenden report:

> Homosexuality is a form of emotional disorder which may cause such grave disruption to the equilibrium of the individual that all meaningful relationships in life are damaged from the outset and peculiarly susceptible to breakdown and destruction. Further, attitudes toward the opposite sex are so filled with distrust, abhorrence, hate, and revulsion as to render them impossible of any relationship except on the most superficial and brittle basis, if then. These characteristics are an outcome of childhood fears which cripple the individual in his total adaptation.

If you want to say that homosexuals are not illegal but just plain hideous, why don't you so state? Fortunately, the Wolfenden Report does not include the kind of degrading addendum you suggest. Why not let it be?

> All male homosexuals suffer, paradoxically, from the yearning to be a man . . .

But they *are* men.

> . . . not a woman, as commonly assumed.

Assumed by whom? You and your group?

> They hope to achieve a "shot" of masculinity in the homosexual act. Ostensibly they may behave in an affectionate and kindly way toward the sexual partner, but this is a veneer, a rationalization to cover the life-saving, ego-saving operation of obligatory homosexuality. The homosexual must carry out his act; unless he does, he will suffer intolerable anxiety and experience massive threat to his psychic organization and functioning. Like the addict, he must have his "fix."

What an ugly appraisal of the sex drive! All you say, despite its abhorrent phraseology, could apply in essence to all human beings who experience strong sexual urges. Certainly heterosexual men caught up in your "Madonna/Prostitute

Syndrome" seem, à la your elegant description, to be getting a "fix." It sounds as though you have an unnatural repugnance for sex—any sex.

> In the light of clinical research, the homosexual symptom can be seen as an intricately designed defense whose purpose is to maintain the equilibrium of a severely disturbed individual. Tampering with his psyche by unqualified persons is to be condemned as he may become seriously disorganized if a premature attempt is made to interrupt his homosexual activities . . .

A heterosexual might well become "seriously disorganized" if an attempt, premature or otherwise, were made to interrupt his heterosexual activities. How would you feel about that?

> . . . conversely, an individual however impelled toward them [homosexual activities], who has refrained from them, may be tragically pushed into them by unwise guidance.

Nobody can either create or un-create a homosexual, any more than create or un-create a heterosexual. Despite your "success stories" of switching around people's sexuality, long-range follow-up discloses that "cures" of homosexuals have not been achieved.

> 5. There is no obligatory homosexual who can be considered healthy. The very existence of this condition precludes it. Despite the appearance at any given time of adequate life performance, there is always extreme conflict present which threatens to disrupt this fragile adjustment.
> 6. As obligatory homosexuality cannot be considered to be a legal issue . . .

Thinking like yours has helped keep it so.

> . . . so it cannot be as a problem of morality. As with

98

psychosis and neurosis, it cannot be regarded as· a consequence of immorality or as a manifestation of evil spirits occupying the body for which special tortures were devised and special legal punishment was exacted.

How can you think of including such a "Dark Ages" expression as "evil spirits occupying the body" in a purportedly scientific paper? As for your "special tortures," even today horrifying "treatments" are being performed on homosexuals. The homosexual press has reported, among other things, that a German neurologist, Hans Orthner of the University of Gottingen, uses an electric probe to deaden, to quote him, "the sex urge center of the brain." This destroys not only brain cells but the patient's memory, along with all sex urges. This doctor reports total success, in that his patients never again indulge in homosexual acts. The September 25, 1970, issue of *Medical World News* seemed well pleased with Dr. Fritz Roeder's method of electrically burning out the homosexual's hypothalamus (part of the brain which is believed to contain vital autonomic nerve centers). How can you and your profession talk about the homosexual's sick, unnatural disorders when medical "crimes" of this kind are being performed?

> These misconceptions must be corrected. It would, however, be the utmost folly to remedy them and then dismiss or overlook the deep psychological disturbance which is the basis of the homosexual condition.

Don't play it again, Sam. All of this would be plain dreary if it were not so menacing.

> Some well-intentioned groups would have us not only do away with legal and moral issues but have us announce the homosexual is not ill at all. They point to disturbances among heterosexuals and attempt to make a comparison.

99

Making comparisons is one of the ways to understanding.

> While the existence of psychosis and neurosis are of course found in heterosexuality, the heterosexual orientation is not of itself an indication of pathological condition while homosexuality always is. The inability to function heterosexually and the extreme hostility toward the opposite sex originating in the fear of one's impulses toward the mother has led to a wholesale flight from the female forever and to a compromise adaptation of choosing a male for sexual gratification and to save the self from intolerable anxiety.

Sam, you played it again. If you want to see "extreme hostility toward the opposite sex" you should attend just one of the many "man-hating" forums conducted by heterosexual women.

> We practice today in the atmosphere of a sweeping sexual revolution. Together with the mainstream heterosexual revolt has come the announcement that a homosexual revolution is also in progress and that homosexuality should be granted total acceptance as a valid form of sexual functioning, different from but equal to heterosexuality. Such acceptance of homosexuality as being a simple variation of normality is naive, not to say grounded in ignorance.

Considering how little knowledge you have displayed, you should try to avoid words such as "naive" and "ignorance." Your theories reveal total lack of familiarity with us, our life styles, and our attitudes.

> Equally misleading is the idea that it is merely an aspect of normal development, a transient stage of adolescence, without meaningful sequelae. That we as physicians could be persuaded to overlook such tendencies among our young people is a harmful fantasy, as shown by the fact that colleges can be pressured to charter homosex-

100

ual groups on campus with all the privileges of other scholastic and social organizations, thereby lending tacit approval.

I have spoken at some of these colleges you mention. Following the talks and the question-and-answer discussions, I have been told by numerous students and teachers, both homosexual and heterosexual, that they began to understand the full scope of homosexuality. I only hope one day we meet on the lecture route.

The implications of such trends are profound. For the adolescent, they make him uncertain and confused.

False. Such trends offer for the first time the opportunity to present information which prevents confusion and uncertainty about homosexuality.

Even for an adult, struggling to strengthen what may be a frail heterosexual organization, the vicissitudes of maintaining sexual adequacy may drive him into a self-despising homosexuality.

If one's heterosexual organization is all that frail, it would most probably be healthier for that person to find out for sure and avoid any further anguish. Better not to conform to an unnatural sexuality than to maladjust to it.

He does not know how else to resolve the deep conflicts which have persisted and tortured him since early childhood. Homosexuality is a foredoomed attempt to find a panacea for the tormenting fear which originated in early childhood and like any unrealistic solution remains unsatisfactory at all times and disastrous much of the time. It is vitally important to realize this fundamental point: the diagnosis of homosexuality cannot be self-made . . .

Do you seriously mean to say that you believe that unless

101

some psychiatrist tells me that I am homosexual I remain in a sexual limbo of identification? Preposterous! Take my word for it: I am a lesbian.

> . . . imposed by jurists, articulated by clergy or speculated about by social scientists. True obligatory homosexuality is a complex condition and has to be differentiated from episodic homosexual behavior entered into for a variety of conscious motivation as stated.

Few of us in the homosexual community have identity problems. The blame for the problems of those of us who do lies at the doors of your and others' institutions.

> If the homosexual is to be granted his human rights as a medical patient . . .

With such "rights" as you describe, I'd rather continue with the social wrongs we fight every day.

> . . . issues which becloud his status should be clarified. Above all the homosexual must be recognized as an individual who presents a medical problem. The whole issue of homosexuality must be transformed into one more scientific challenge to medicine which has time and again been able to alleviate the plaguing illnesses of man. With this respected leadership on the part of the physician, we will see a surge of support for the study and treatment of the disorder by all techniques and knowledge available through the great resources and medical talent of the United States.

With a "friendly expert" like you, Dr. Socarides, who needs enemies?

Some of the other "experts" may on the surface seem to be less rabid than Dr. Socarides; but on examination, one learns that they have for the most part the same views. In

102

the April 1971 issue of *Sexual Behavior,* Dr. Harvey Kaye wrote:

> I shall purposely dodge the terms "sick" and "neurotic." They have unfortunately acquired such a pejorative con- notation in our culture that a rational consideration is made all but impossible. . . . I believe that homosexual- ity in women is not a conscious and chosen preference. It is a reaction to a crippling inhibition of heterosexual development. . . . This reaction is then interwoven with other patterns such as a group of lesbian friends and the lesbian subculture, which leads to a more drastic adjust- ment. Essentially, the heterosexual drive is inhibited by anxieties and threats which make a heterosexual adap- tation all but impossible [author's note: again, all of this is leading toward the either-conform-or-maladjust approach, and those who don't "conform" remain psy- chiatric "cripples"]. A major criterion in any medical decision to "treat" a condition is the impairment or in- hibition of function. For example, arthritis is a condi- tion which merits treatment since the function of one or several joints of the body is impaired. Since I view homosexuality, in part, as an inhibition of the hetero- sexual function, the treatment of homosexuality then becomes a legitimate consideration. Furthermore, since there is an impairment of function—that is the homo- sexual individual *cannot,* rather than simply *chooses* not to relate well heterosexually—the "normal varia- tion" argument does not sit comfortably with me. In addition, the interpersonal conflict and personal un- happiness found among homosexuals cannot, to my mind, be attributed entirely to a society's stigmatization of homosexuality. Rather, most often it seems born of emotional disturbance and perpetuates such disurbance.

It is clear that although Dr. Kaye "dodges" the terms "sick" and "neurotic" he still ends up using them, albeit

103

euphemistically: "crippling inhibition," "arthritic condi-tion," "emotional disturbance," and so on.

Actually, it is difficult to find psychiatrists and psychologists who do not regard homosexuality as a sickness and who do treat homosexuals by helping them adjust to their situation in a society which is overtly hostile. At our D.O.B. discussion on lesbianism and psychiatry, some young women reported that their parents had gone to the library to "read up" on homosexuality when they "suspected" their daughters' orientation. And, of course, it was the Socarideses, Biebers, and Kayes they found on the shelves. Often the young women agreed to go to psychiatrists, who, in most cases, pressed, shamed, and frightened them into believing that heterosexuality was the only "cure" for their homosexuality. But anywhere from a few months to a few years later, these confused and often emotionally scarred lesbians came to D.O.B. and, in relief, began rehabilitation to their natural life style.

There are doctors who will work with adults who are avowed homosexuals. But let a very young woman walk in, and usually the entire emphasis is to lead or shove her into heterosexuality. D.O.B. had a referral service for those of its members who felt they needed help (religious, medical, and employment areas were covered). Dr. Sharon London worked with our organization and was able to help a number of women. Saint Vincent's Hospital in New York City has a good overall policy of working with homosexuals; however, it does depend on the individual doctor. Dr. Helen Kaplan, who heads the Payne Whitney Psychiatric Division of Cornell Medical Center, would also be helpful. Dr. Kaplan invited me, along with a few other homosexuals, to speak there for two consecutive years and she seemed to have an enlightened attitude toward homosexuality.

104

In practically every part of the country there are homosexual organizations and women's centers which have referral services. A lesbian who believes she might be helped by therapy should contact these local groups. In some cases, therapists with positive approaches to lesbianism are available.

In no wise do I urge therapy, except for those women who feel a desperate need for it. The best "therapy" I know is getting into the homosexual community, working either behind the scenes (for those still closeted) or actively. I have seen many women who were helped more by this than by any other method. There is joy in learning that you are not alone, that there are many who live the homosexual life in dignity and happiness.

We have examined the overwhelmingly negative attitude of the psychiatric profession toward homosexuals. It has also been observed that its attitude toward lesbianism has exhausted little of the doctors' time or energies, since lesbians have pretty much been ignored. One need only read Dr. Phyllis Chesler's personal account (in *Women and Madness*) of the damage the profession has done to women as a class to understand its attitude about women in general.

It is clear that women as a group represent the profession's best customers, since this is a profession which adamantly endorses and demands of its patients adherence to the church/state, law-of-nature dictate which has kept women oppressed for centuries. In effect, the medical profession acts as the scientific Good Housekeeping Seal of Approval for the Church's and other societal institutions' structuring of our culture.

Psychiatrists have been generally successful in maintaining their stand that lesbians are "inferior" to heterosexual women because lesbians set aside our culture's "natural"

105

standards of sexual role, which, of course, places them at the bottom of the hierarchy of their class—women.

In recent years it has become increasingly obvious that some women in the feminist movement have discarded the psychiatric profession's "rules" regarding woman's role. Now they must learn that they should embrace lesbianism, if not as a personal issue, certainly as a political one, if only to show that they will not allow the profession which oppresses them to separate them from their lesbian sisters.

Other oppressed groups also must get past the propaganda which they have been spoon-fed—by the very same institutions which have oppressed them—and regard us not with fear or anxiety but rather as a political force whose numbers are large, whose numbers cross all minority group lines.

The psychiatric profession as a whole is instrumental in maintaining the oppression of homosexuals. It is also responsible for isolating us from other groups by erroneous and loathsome "theories," "treatments," and alleged cures. It gets widespread and frequent representation in our country's mass media, where it is given further opportunity to carry its message, to reinforce its concepts.

And yet despite all this, more and more of us in the homosexual community are proving that it is healthier to adjust to our natural heritage than it is to attempt, unsuccessfully, to conform and maladjust to what our institutions have defined as woman's and man's roles.

7

Homosexuals—In and Out of the News
Mass Media's Funny Funnel

> *"There are scenes in the following program which may shock you. I tell you this in advance in case you don't wish to watch it or don't want your children to see it."*
> —*Announcement by Edwin R. Newman prior to the NBC television network program, "New York Illustrated, Homosexuals: Out of the Closet." February 18, 1973.*

The above network television announcement is unusual, since it preceded a program which included nothing "shocking." Basically, the program (which was sponsored by the Chase Manhattan Bank) presented interviews with a few homosexuals, both men and women, and with New York Councilman Carter Burden. It showed brief filmed segments of social events at the Gay Activists Alliance Firehouse and short interludes taken from meetings there. There were also some scenes shot in a gay bar, which actually should have removed some of the heterosexual anxiety about "what goes on in places like that." It became clear that, in fact, nothing goes on in "places like that" that is any different from what goes on in other bars. Bruce Voeller, then president of Gay Activists Alliance, Michael Miller of the Gay Legal Caucus, and several women discussed their lives and goals, and in a couple of instances displayed casual, warm affection for their partners.

No, there was nothing "shocking" on the show, despite that ominous warning and the fact that Mr. Newman made statements during his narration such as "Homosexuality treads on the central nervous system of our society"—which ought to get some prize in the mixed metaphor category. There was no violence, no obscenity, no ugliness of the sort viewers see on shows such as "Patton" ("We are going to go through that field like crap through a goose!") or "All in the Family" ("spade," "kike," "spic," "fag") or so many other ill-conceived programs which assault the intelligence and aesthetic values of their audiences. None of these programs is prefaced by any such warning.

In the nearly twenty years I spent in the public relations field (including work in some of the country's top agencies, such as J. Walter Thompson, N. W. Ayer, Harshe-Rotman & Druck, and Hill & Knowlton, among others), I had the opportunity to witness firsthand precisely how mass media can be manipulated. To understand the problem one must first differentiate between advertising and public relations. Advertising is paid-for space in print media or commercial time on radio and television. Any company or organization with the means can buy space and present whatever message, verbally or pictorially, it wishes (as long as it meets F.C.C. standards, i.e., truth in advertising, etc.). Public relations is a process whereby a story, sometimes accompanied by a visual about a company's product(s), services, or image, is developed in such a way that an editor feels it has value to readers or viewers from a news, human interest, or other point of view. A public relations story, or publicity, is not paid for by the business or organization. It is what is called "free space" or "free time."

108

Many years ago there was a distinct division between editorial and advertising staffs of the media. And it would have been a breach of public relations etiquette to mention an advertising campaign of the company for which the publicist was conducting a public relations program. The editor's obligation was to decide on use of the material in question on the basis of its merit alone. The editor guarded her editorial sanction from commercialism and from other external pressure.

This situation has changed radically during the last twenty or so years. Today many editors will immediately ask a publicist, "Does your client *advertise* with us?"

To give an example, a few years ago I was asked by my then boss to send to *The New York Times* a release about the engagement of the niece of an important public relations client. Since all newspapers have certain space limitations they cannot carry all such announcements and photos. The *Times* did not run the release and the head of my agency got back to me with, "Call them back and tell them that she is the niece of Mr. So-and-So, who is head of X Company. They are heavy advertisers. Put some pressure on." The *Times* ran the release and photograph the next day.

This example, blatant though benign, basically illustrates the bind in which the editorial staffs of media find themselves.

What news gets printed or shown, and in what light ("slanting the news"), depends on all kinds of pressures, be they business, political, or moral. Mr. Newman's warning, juxtaposing a word such as "shock" and a program on homosexuality (when nothing "shocking" took place on the show), is one method of slanting the news. Editorial jurisdiction has been brought to bear on the opinion of the audience; in effect, before the program is presented, editorial

109

"sanction," by way of approval of the program content, is denied. Why? The media may have been affected by the widespread negative views of our cultural institutions; perhaps the network felt it should keep in step with the majority view on homosexuality. Or it may be that when the network decided to put together the program it was influenced by "experts" on homosexuality. Or maybe it was simply an audience-retaining ploy. I can hear someone in the station's promotion department saying, "Hey, that's good —it'll keep 'em from switching channels!" Or perhaps the program's sponsor insisted on the "face-saving" preface, to make sure the "stigma" of homosexuality would not be related in the viewers' minds to Chase Manhattan. There is no way of knowing which influences from which sources were involved. One may be pretty sure, however, that the warning was not solely the invention of Mr. Newman.

Another method of slanting the news involves repeated presentation of one side of an issue, with only rare presentation of the other side, which happens continually when homosexuality is involved. Still another way of slanting the news is for the media finally to pretend to represent the other side while actually maintaining a biased viewpoint. One example of this technique is *The New York Times Magazine* feature on D.O.B., "The Disciples of Sappho, Updated," by Judy Klemesrud, in the March 28, 1971, edition.

Judy had promised that I would be sent proofs of the piece before it went to the printer, so that I could make any changes or correct any errors. Strangely, the story went to the printer early and I had no opportunity to see it before it came out in print (with errors intact). Earlier, however, Judy had called me to say the *Times* board of editors had accepted the story, but only on the condition that Judy include "three anti-homosexual quotes from psychiatrists."

When I asked why, she said that "on the basis of presenting both sides," her editors felt the story needed "balance." I reminded her that as recently as the previous Wednesday, the *Times* had run the story "Homosexuality: Parents Aren't Always to Blame," a gross misrepresentation of homosexuality, with no concern to "present both sides." Where had the board's "editorial ethics" been hiding when it printed, as it had done repeatedly in the past, totally anti-homosexual articles?

Judy asked if I could recommend psychiatrists who might be able to give her the quotes she needed. I told her to check out the previous Wednesday's paper and all the other anti-homosexual articles her publication had run.

While researching her story, Judy had attended our D.O.B. meetings and a dance, and spent three hours interviewing me in my home. She spent many hours with other lesbian women, and she spoke of the warmth and friendship D.O.B. had inspired in her. Yet in her article she dismissed the political value of the D.O.B. Lesbian Center; its function in the homosexual and feminist communities was passed over. There were statements made that were erroneous. For example, the feature began, "As recently as a year ago, most members of the New York chapter of Daughters of Bilitis, the country's oldest and largest lesbian organization, knew each other only by first names, which were usually false." This simply is not true. To my knowledge, only one member was then using a false first name. Judy went on to say, "Meetings in a small, stuffy, sublet room on West 38th Street were uninspiring and poorly attended." It's true the space was small and stuffy; but D.O.B.'s meetings, according to Kay Tobin and Randy Wicker, the authors of *The Gay Crusaders*, "were some of the most exciting held in New York." For example, it was at D.O.B. that Ti-Grace Atkinson

111

spoke to a group of well over two hundred women, the first time the feminist political theorist had ever addressed a lesbian organization; it was at D.O.B. that Kate Millett spoke to a crowd of equal size and "came out." She said, among other things, "It has taken me a long time, but I am finally here; I have finally come home." (In the D.O.B. Newsletter which covered Kate's speech the editor wrote, "She changed some heads at D.O.B.; somebody said, 'Hearing Kate Millett had more therapeutic value than twenty sessions with a shrink!' ") Dr. Phyllis Chesler spoke to a very large crowd of women and discussed some of the personal problems women have in relationship to psychiatrists, a subject she later expanded in her book *Women and Madness*. No, the meetings were not "uninspiring and poorly attended."

Judy began the second paragraph of the story with, "Today, although they are still in the 'Establishment' lesbian group . . ." "Establishment"? We were involved in many kinds of political actions and demonstrations, as well as keeping a solid "social" program going for those who were looking primarily for the support of belonging to a group. What was her source for this conclusion, I wonder.

The *Times* article resulted in a lot of interest in D.O.B., but the treatment of the organization by the *Times* and the implication of that treatment had to be acknowledged and clarified. The article gave much space to psychiatrists who viewed homosexuals as basically sick, or, as Dr. Harvey Kaye said in the feature, "arthritic fingers."

Some of the women in the organization made comments such as, "Well, at least they are *talking* about us," or, "But, it's marvelous publicity and we mustn't be rude to the press, or ungrateful." Such remarks are rationalizations, which avoid the responsibility of analyzing the function and intent of the mass media as a whole.

112

Another example of exploitation of homosexuals took place in April 1971 and involved the "Bandy Show."

On April 5, 1971, the associate producer of the show, Dolores Danska, asked me to appear with Jill Johnston (writer for the *Village Voice* and author of *Lesbian Nation*), Dr. Charles Socarides, and Dr. Harvey Kaye. I went to the station for an exploratory interview with Mrs. Danska and strongly expressed my view that the proposed panel was totally out of balance. I said that I found Mr. Bandy notably oppressive to his guests—certainly not an impartial moderator; Jill, at that time, was not in my opinion a strong feminist ally, having expressed anti-woman views in her columns (she has, since those days, tempered her views substantially). I suggested the format be a one-to-one confrontation between a psychiatrist and a lesbian, no matter who that lesbian might be.

Dolores said that she would consider making such a change, and in fact asked Ellen Povill, then vice-president of D.O.B., to come to the station for an interview the following day. Following the interview with Ellen, Mrs. Danska said that she definitely wanted Ellen to be on the show, but she would have to check with the producer. I called her late in the afternoon on Wednesday and she said that they had decided to follow the original plan for the show.

I met with a few D.O.B. members, including Ti-Grace, to discuss the problem: *TV Guide* was to carry my name in the listing for the "Bandy Show," and if I refused to be on the show it could be made to appear as a "cop-out." We decided that I would appear on the show, but would refuse to discuss lesbianism from the point of view of "defending" it. I would attempt to address myself solely to the collusion between the media and the psychiatrists. This collusion was

113

blatantly evident with respect to the feminist movement (the press quoted psychiatric opinion to the effect that feminists were troubled women unable to adjust to their roles as wives and mothers). Similar collusion had been used against blacks during their struggle (militant blacks were said to be paranoid and expressing repressed hostilities).

I called Dolores just prior to the taping and asked if a few D.O.B. members could participate from the audience during the question-and-answer segment of the program. She said they could. Ti-Grace called people in the press to cover the show. She reached Helen Dudar of the *New York Post,* who was unable to go to the station herself, but arranged for *Post* reporter Dick Schwartz to be present.

Ellen, Ti-Grace, Eileen Webb, Lyn Kypferman, Maricla Moyano, and I arrived at the station early. Dolores informed us that the format of the show was to be in four segments: one, Jill and John Bandy; two, Dr. Socarides and me; three, Bandy, Johnston, Socarides, Kaye, Povill, and Simpson; and, four, questions from the audience. I had a quick conference with the D.O.B. women. It was clear that from this point on improvisation would be necessary.

As we were called to the on-stage area, I asked if I might sit in the audience during the first segment. This was arranged.

BANDY: Tonight we are going to talk about women who love other women.

RUTH: (rising from the audience and walking to the small circular stage) No, tonight we are going to have a very creative show. Tonight we are going to talk about the collusion of the media and the psychiatric profession.

BANDY: Who are you?

RUTH: I am Ruth Simpson, your other lesbian guest. (Neither Ellen nor I had met Bandy as of this time.)

114

At this point Ellen came up onto the stage and was introduced by me.

BANDY: Miss Simpson, what do you mean by collusion?

I explained what I meant. Bandy turned immediately and began questioning Jill on her marriage and her two children. I said to Jill that she didn't have to answer such questions, that lesbianism did not need to be defended on this level. Jill said that she agreed with what we were doing, but nevertheless she answered Bandy, who said, "There, you see, Miss Johnston, you answered that quite well." I said, "Mr. Bandy, are you always this condescending to your guests?"

Bandy asked me why we had not told him what D.O.B. had planned to do on the show. Ti-Grace volunteered from the audience, "You don't tell your battle strategy to the enemy." Bandy remarked that our tactics were rude and Ellen said, "If you act like Nazis, we will treat you like Nazis," referring to Dr. Socarides' suggested detention camps for homosexuals.

Bandy then asked me why I would not discuss lesbianism with the psychiatrists and I asked him how he would feel about someone in the black movement being asked to discuss their treatment by whites with two or three Grand Dragons of the Ku Klux Klan. He didn't answer.

Again, Ellen and I, with help from Ti-Grace in the audience, pursued the collusion theme until the show stopped taping for a commercial. The executive producer requested that our "women should be reasonable," adding that there would be no psychiatrists on the show if Jill and I would continue the interview with Bandy, but that Ellen would have to leave the stage.

"Presenting a balance, presenting both sides was simply part of their policy," Mrs. Danska said. "Why, yes," she added, "we plan to do a show like that on the assassination

115

of Dr. King. We plan to present both sides there, too." My mind still reels when I think of her remark.

We were asked again to do the show—without the psychiatrists. The obvious problem, we pointed out, was that the producers could, if they wished, tape the psychiatrists separately and edit the tape, splicing in their interviews (quoting out of context is one of the most insidious methods of distorting the news). The executive producer said that we would just have to take his word for it that this would not be done. Ti-Grace insisted that we would have to have the promise in writing. He refused to provide a written agreement.

Ellen and I turned to Jill and asked her to leave with us and the other D.O.B. women. She said that she would "stay and do the best I can."

We insisted that the releases we had signed be returned to us. Here is an extract of that release:

Date: April 7, 1971

Metromedia Television
Division of Metromedia, Inc.
205 East 67th Street
New York, N. Y. 10021

Gentlemen:

I hereby agree to your recording and broadcasting my appearance and/or participation on your television program entitled: *John Bandy* and in consideration of the mutual benefits flowing therefrom, I agree as follows:

1. You are the sole owner of all rights in and to the Program and the contents and recordings thereof for all purposes and uses whatsoever including without limitation, the right throughout the world and forever to broadcast or license for broadcast the Program and/or recordings thereof one or more times over any and all

116

stations on a commercial and/or sustaining basis, the right to publish, disseminate, and edit the text of the Program in any form and to assign all or part of any such rights to others. . . .

Reluctantly the releases were returned and we left.

Dick Schwartz, the *Post* reporter, called me twice late that night to check on quotes from the doctors; he said that "the story was going to be real good." He left the *Post* at 2:30 A.M., after his last call to me, leaving the story and a long memo for his editor on the uniqueness of the event. But Bob Spitzler, a *Post* editor, "bumped" the story. It did not run. No explanation.

The resulting show was not telecast, and shortly thereafter, the "Bandy Show" was removed from the station's programming.

Early in 1971, the "Dear Abby" column carried this item: "To those who wrote to blast me for my refusal to put down the homosexual: The most burdensome problem the homosexual must bear is the stigma placed upon him by an unenlightened and intolerant society. Their sexual bent is as natural and normal for them as ours is for us. They are neither 'sick' nor degenerate. They are simply different. Mine is a plea for compassion and understanding for these misunderstood and mistreated souls. They, too, are God's children."

Such a statement is like a gust of fresh air, cutting through the pollution of myth-wishes, and we who were at D.O.B. at the time realized how dear Abby was in this instance.

With a few scattered exceptions, however, literature on homosexuality has reflected the myth-wishes of our culture. The homosexual is, among other things, killed by a falling tree (*The Fox*); commits suicide (*Girls in Uniform* and

The Children's Hour); goes insane *(The Well of Loneliness);* finds Mr. Right, or thinks she has *(Diana);* at end of book or final curtain is desolate and alone *(The Boys in the Band* or *That Certain Summer).* Then there are all of the junk books which use homosexuality to titillate, exploiting us in boring or degrading situations.

There are some exceptions in homosexual literature—two notable ones: *The Price of Salt,* in which the lesbians are separated but at the close of the book are reunited, and Isabel Miller's *Patience and Sara,* which is loved and admired by the lesbian community, since it speaks truthfully of a natural lesbian relationship. *Small Changes,* a powerful novel by Marge Piercy, is an account of one woman's attempt to discover her true sexual identity.

ABC-TV's "That Certain Summer" is interesting since it combines two media, literature and television. In his *New York Post* column "On the Air" which previewed the show, Bob Williams wrote:

> Seldom if ever in viewing history has a network taken such elaborate precautions with a program as ABC is taking to cushion the impact Nov. 1 of a made-for-TV movie, "That Certain Summer," which deals with homosexuality.
> The subject of the third sex has been relatively untouched in network dramatics and the obvious worry is how it will set with the little old lady from Dubuque. [Note: actually, we had a D.O.B. member who was an elderly woman from Dubuque.] Accordingly, the film is being screened in advance before virtually everybody in an opinion-making capacity who might object. It could become the most pretested show ever.
> Virtually every sponsor agency buying time for blurbs on the network's Movie of the Week series has passed judgment on the film, without protest. Yesterday, the network screened the movie via closed-circuit to affil-

iated stations across the country, without immediate complaints over the subject matter.

Meanwhile, the screenings go on here, as well as in Los Angeles, with invited guests ranging from clergymen to housewives, show-biz types, non show-biz types and, yes, gay activists. The pre-telecast audience for the film must be running into the thousands.

"Homosexuality," explained a network spokesman, "is a very sensitive subject. We don't know what the reaction is going to be around the country. The subject is new on television. It hasn't been treated at all in major dramatic length or form."

William Link, who wrote and co-produced the film with Richard Levinson, said the preview cards were being handed out to Hollywood screening room customers. Ninety-five percent of them, he said, voted affirmatively for the movie. . . .

The percentage is hardly surprising, since the story is that of a homosexual man, divorced and the father of a fourteen-year-old son, who is living with his homosexual partner. When his son comes to visit him, that certain summer, he is forced to explain his homosexuality to his son. During his embarrassed and abject "confession" he calls his condition "sick." His son leaves in an upset and hostile state with his mother, who has come to get him.

This situation naturally fits the cultural image of how "harmful" and "destructive" homosexuality is. Mr. Williams' column continues:

> . . . With minor reservations, we had to regard it as one of those rare made-for-TV movies which ought to be called a TV drama. The network TV merchants, of course, are hesitant to call a TV show by its rightful name, a TV show. They'd rather play the "movie" game. The problem with the made-for-TV movie is that most of them are designed as pilot films for new crime series,

119

> such as are now cluttering the TV screen. "The safest thing we can do," said one network programming chief the other night, "is just to keep giving people another crime-show."
>
> "That Certain Summer" breaks away from the crime mold of the made-for-TV movie rather strikingly. The concerned treatment of the plight of the homosexual in heretofore timid TV drama series is distinctive and worth attention when the show comes up on the screen Nov. 1.

The play-drama-movie—whatever it might be called—was, it is true, beautifully filmed, was well paced, and showed a reasonably good homosexual relationship between two men; however, it culminated in the usual "debacle." During the protagonist's final talk with his son he changed from a good and sensitive father to a floundering, nonsupportive, and confused man—a situation that fits the public attitude that homosexuality is basically an unfortunate illness. Because the show was "sensitive," the viewer was offered the additional luxury of feeling safe in her or his own "normalcy," and feeling sorry for, therefore superior to, the poor homosexual. No one felt seriously threatened since the homosexual's place in the pecking order had not been changed.

In his *Times* review of *That Certain Summer,* John J. O'Connor wrote: "Whatever the conclusion, the whole persisted in maintaining for its central homosexual character a context that was rigorously 'normal,' if not verging on saintliness. It was this aspect of the production that might have shocked some viewers."

It really makes you wonder—"damned if you do and damned if you don't," seems to be the exitless labyrinth to which society condemns the homosexual. There is evidence all around us that bigotry is prevalent in our society, but there is a subtle (to the heterosexual) and obvious (to the homosexual) difference in the bigotry directed at homosexuals. Since homosexuality is generally viewed as a sin against nature, the public is used to sniggering at it. This difference in attitude is expressed in the following, which appeared in the February 25, 1973, edition of *The New York Times*.

"BIGOTED"

To The Editor:

We agree with Jack Paar ("Will Johnny Be Up to Paar?") that "every time you tell a kid a word like 'spade' you haven't accomplished anything good." One word that Paar himself seems addicted to is "fairy." Let him try it out on some of the homosexuals he knows, and describes as "enormously talented people of great dignity."

We guess that those of us in the Gay movement he calls "amateur fairies" will have to go on battling until "professionals" like Paar are forced to shut their bigoted yaps—in print and on the airwaves. We clocked an average of five anti-homosexual jokes on each of his first week's shows. Paar, we think, is not the fellow to talk about dignity.

Bruce Voeller
President,
Gay Activists Alliance

New York City

Homosexuals are so often fair game for ridicule because our image of "queer" or "sick" is perpetuated by those in authority. Until that image is changed, that is until a prejudiced society learns to accept homosexuality not as a deviation from the so-called "norm" but as a norm in its own right, that bigotry will remain a part of our daily lives.

121

8

Lesbians and Law Enforcement
They're Only Lesbians ...
Until They Begin to Organize

In September 1970, shortly after becoming president of D.O.B. New York, I received a telephone call at the public relations agency where I worked. The call was from Sergeant Kelly of the 14th Precinct; he asked if I was president of D.O.B. I told him I was. He announced: "We are doing a check of your organization and we need some information." I asked him where he had gotten my business telephone number; he volunteered that "we have our ways." (At this point I already knew that my home telephone was being tapped, and obviously D.O.B.'s phone was too.) I asked him why he was investigating our organization and for whom. He gave me the "this is just a routine check" explanation which has been used so many times with those whom the law wishes to intimidate. He said, "I want the numbers of your charter and certificate of authority." I explained that our legal papers were in the office of our lawyer and gave him the lawyer's name and telephone number.

When he asked if I couldn't give him the numbers "right away," I said, "You know that you are calling me on my job, and you must realize that I don't carry D.O.B.'s legal papers around with me." He asked, "What about the occupancy sign for the premises where you meet?" I responded, "What about it?" Then I explained that D.O.B. at that time sublet space from the Corduroy Club (a male homosexual social club) and that the Corduroy Club, not D.O.B., was responsible for the sign. I also said that the men there had already told me that police had been to see them the week before and that he certainly must know of our sublet arrangement with the Corduroy Club.

At the end of the conversation I called our lawyer, described my conversation, and said to please let me know about any call from Kelly.

Having heard nothing for a few days, I called the lawyer again to see if the call had come in. It had not. At the D.O.B. meeting the following Thursday, I told the women in attendance about the call and said that we would probably start to get police harassment (we knew that other homosexual organizations were being "visited" by cops).

One week later, a D.O.B. planning session attended by about fifty women was interrupted when two uniformed cops entered without knocking. I went toward them quickly and told them that they were on our premises illegally and asked for their names and badge numbers. Their names were Sergeant Kelly and Patrolman Fierro. Their attitudes were hostile. Fierro had his "squawk box" going at full volume. Kelly asked to see our certificate of authority and charter. I asked why he had not called our lawyer as I had suggested when he called me two weeks prior. He said he had tried many times to reach the lawyer but "nobody answered the phone." I told him that this was difficult to believe since the lawyer was a partner in a large new firm with a switchboard and secretaries. Kelly said maybe it was hard to believe but it was so. I asked Fierro to turn down his squawk box; he refused. Kelly then asked for the occupancy sign, and I again explained that it was not our responsibility but that of the Corduroy Club. I repeatedly said that they had no right to enter our meeting or ask to see anything or anybody. At this point I became anxious about possible arrests, since neither cop had shown anything other than ugly hostility. I worried about the women there since any whose jobs required a state license (teacher, lawyer, doctor, beautician, taxi driver, etc.) could, if arrested, have their licenses revoked (by New York State law homosexuals are deemed to be "of bad moral character" and may not hold state licenses); I was also very worried about those who might have come to D.O.B. for the first time and might be traumatized, those who were closeted and might suffer long-term negative results from an arrest. When asked what D.O.B. had done and why the cops were interested in us, Fierro said, "Oh, I think you know what you've done." This sounded threatening, and I became even more apprehensive for the women. When some of the women began saying things like, "No, we don't know what we've done, please tell us," I said, "Sisters, please let me as officer in charge talk with them."

Sergeant Kelly asked for my personal identification and when I refused he said, "Get your coat—we're taking you in to the station." Ellen, who was then vice-president of D.O.B., had gone into the office at the back of the room to phone our lawyer.

The women were wonderful—a number of them said, in effect, "If you take her you take us, too." And most of them were prepared to go. As the cops and I walked toward the door I stopped and said, "I *will* talk to our lawyer before I go with you."

Sergeant Kelly turned, faced me, with his nightstick in front of him, one end held in each hand, and said, "I don't really want to have to break your horn." I said, "You *what?*" He would not repeat it. At this point Ellen came out of the office and said that she had our lawyer on the phone. Kelly told me to take the call. I was advised by the lawyer to show ID, otherwise, "They might take you in and you might end up in the House of D (the Women's House of Detention) and you might get pretty badly hassled." I gave the cops my driver's license.

Kelly wrote out a summons (the "offense" on the summons was "Occupancy signs") and ordered me to appear in court for a hearing at 9:30 A.M. on October 23, and they both left.

Working with other homosexual organizations, D.O.B. planned a demonstration on the morning of the hearing, which was to be at the 100 Centre Street Court House. We also asked for media coverage of the event. I talked with the mayor's office, in accordance with the offer from City Hall to homosexual organizations to "call with your problems." (David Lebenstein, who was on the staff there at that time, said: "Actually, the Mayor knows that his office has lost control of the police department at precinct level." Not very reassuring!) I further informed the American Civil Liberties Union of the police action and the homosexual community's intention to fight the harassment.

On the morning of the hearing and demonstration, the courtroom was changed at the last minute to one at 52 Chambers Street; as a result, the media and some of the homosexuals coming to demonstrate couldn't find the demonstration. However, homosexual sisters and brothers filled the courtroom, and when the judge called my name, they all stood in silent protest. Those who joined D.O.B. that day included members from Gay Liberation Front, Gay Activists Alliance, Radicalesbians, Street Transvestites Action Revolutionaries, Homophile Action League, Gay Youth, Mattachine, and the Christopher Street Liberation Day Committee.

Sergeant Kelly was not in court that day.

I pleaded not guilty and was told that I would be notified by mail of the date of my trial.

For those who are uninitiated in the area of police harassment—even harassment of this relatively mild form—it should be noted that court appearances for such harassment charges are very time-consuming and expensive for the organization or individual involved. Ultimately, I had to appear in court twice more on this charge, and three times on subsequent harassment charges against D.O.B. (excluding, of course, the additional times I went to courtrooms in support of others undergoing similar ordeals).

Fortunately, I had already told my employer that I am a homosexual; however, having to take days off from a job does not make for a very good employer-employee relationship. One's case may not be called until afternoon of the day of either the hearing or trial, and if the arresting or summons-giving cop does not appear in the courtroom, the case is postponed. Those who talk piously about case overloads in the courts might direct their attention to the many cops who add to this burden by failing to appear, adding also to the harassment of the "defendants." And our Constitution notwithstanding, one is truly presumed guilty until proved innocent.

This initial charge was ultimately dismissed, but later there were others. Three cops, including two sergeants, came to D.O.B.'s Lesbian Center on Prince Street during a party. I was not there that night, but home resting, having spent day and night for several months helping to get the Center together. Ellen was in charge of the women's dance that night. She called me to say that the cops had come. They had pushed her clear across the floor of our very large loft when she told them that unless they had a search warrant they could not come in. I got to D.O.B. in less than ten minutes. By this time women were beginning to arrive for the party, so we stationed a woman downstairs to tell those entering that the police were upstairs—if they were frightened for their jobs, for their citizenship (naturalized citizenship can be denied or revoked on the charge of homosexuality), or for any other reason, they should not come into the Center. By this time we had also worked out a system of alerting the Gay Activists Alliance, which had just opened their Firehouse meeting place around the corner from D.O.B. We had "runners" so that if cops came to D.O.B. we would send someone to GAA to warn them that cops would probably arrive there soon, and vice versa. We sent a woman to GAA to alert them. Sergeants Carbonara and Foster and Patrolman Petermann stayed on our premises illegally for more than an hour, hostile and threatening. Petermann issued three summonses to me, "violation of licenses," "no permit—place of assembly," and "no certificate of occupancy" were the charges this time. In the course of this particular harassment I asked Sgt. Carbonara, in front of many witnesses, if he planned to be in court on the day of the trial. He said, "You can know that I won't be in court —I wouldn't waste my time that way." When I said that represented obvious harassment, he said, "Well, that's life."

I asked him why the police department doesn't make similar visits to P.T.A.'s or other nonprofit organizations? Why,

I asked, if we were D.A.R. and not D.O.B. would we *not* receive threatening and destructive harassing "attention" from the police department? He said, smirking, "Now you don't really have to ask that, do you?"

Then I asked him why, when there were muggings, rapes, robberies, and murders going on throughout the city, three "members of the force" had spent this much time on people who were involved in no illegalities whatever. He said, "Listen you, we are only doing what we are told." When I asked him *who* told them, he refused to answer.

Jim Owles, then president of GAA, and a couple of other brothers came over to see if there were going to be arrests. Sensitive to the feminist aspects of the situation, he said that he figured we would want to handle this on our own, but that if things "got rough" GAA could send some men over to "help out." I thanked them for coming and said that we would handle it ourselves.

I asked the cops if they ever pay similar calls to the campaign headquarters of political candidates, and Carbonara said, "I would if I didn't like them politically." I said, "Oh, then you would be making a personal decision. It wouldn't simply be a matter of 'only doing what you were told' in that instance." At that point he said, "Listen you, don't talk smart!"

After issuing me the three summonses they left, but with the promise that they "would return later that night." When I asked why, they refused to answer.

They did not come back that night, but they did return again. And again. The last time they came to D.O.B., in the fall of 1971—after I had left the organization and it no longer had the Prince Street loft—many uniformed cops and some plainclothes detectives appeared suddenly. According to one of the women who were arrested that night,

"I couldn't begin to tell you how many of them there were. There were six police cars, and they were swarming all over the place." That night at D.O.B. the police dumped large containers holding ice cubes, soft drinks, and beer all over the floor; generally messed up D.O.B.'s quarters, destroying property; and arrested two women, taking them into the precinct and holding them for about four hours. The charge was "selling beer without a license." It should be explained that D.O.B. as a nonprofit educational organization was legally authorized to give beers and sodas to members and friends for small donations. The cops knew that this was a fraudulent charge, since the issue of the beer and soda, and the fact that we were not profiting from its sale, had come up repeatedly during their previous "visits," as well as during telephone calls I had made to precincts, to commanding officers of precincts, and to the mayor's office.

This charge and all other charges against D.O.B. were ultimately dropped, but only after the usual number of court appearances, the wasted time of many, the expense to D.O.B., and arrest records for the women involved.

It should be noted that a relatively short while after this last case of harassment, D.O.B. stopped functioning as an organization. As of this writing, it has not restructured itself. That there is a connection between police harassment and the disintegration of minority group organizations cannot be seriously doubted; it has happened too often to be coincidental. Such harassment is a well-known and often-used method of intimidation which also discourages new memberships and supporters.

Harassment of individuals is another way of "dampening" the spirit of those in minority groups. The following are some examples of this sort of harassment:

First, it must be understood that what men do in our culture is usually considered more important than what women do; therefore, male homosexuals are apt to receive more physical harassment than do women because their "deviate sexual acts" are considered "more important." It is not unusual for male homosexuals to be picked up by police, driven around in the back of cop cars, insulted verbally and physically, often badly beaten, sometimes dumped out of the car, sometimes taken to the station, held for a while and then released—usually no charges are made. If they are, they are almost always dropped later.

At the State Assembly hearing on victimless crimes at which Ellen and I testified on January 7, 1971, Bob Kohler of the Gay Community Center (which no longer exists, having gone the way of D.O.B. and some other homosexual organizations) testified as follows: "A gay, a friend of mine, was held in a pig precinct—he was handcuffed to a radiator for six hours. He had a gash in his head, inflicted by pigs, which later required eight stitches. He was handcuffed to this fucking radiator for six hours with a nightstick up his ass." Bob went on to say that there were many instances which he could cite of similar brutality inflicted on homosexuals for no reason other than some cop or cops had the "suspicion" that they might be homosexual. At another victimless crimes hearing, Joseph L. Norton, Ph.D. in psychology, noted:

> The fact that he is illegal makes the homosexual unable to seek the protection of the law. Last New Year's Eve two suburban neighbors of mine were discussing how some older, rougher acquaintances of theirs in the Bronx used to go "queer popping": getting a homosexual to make an advance to one of them, then as a group ganging up on him. These older boys, some of them college students. [sic] These boys knew they could be vicious because the homosexual had no recourse.

130

Our dilemma should be clear: even as victims we have no recourse for fighting violations of our persons and psyches —we can't call a cop!

News of this situation travels fast in oppressed minorities, and it is not conducive to participation in political organizations by members of those minorities.

Blacks are familiar with unequal treatment under the law; they understand the irony of having no option for legal protection against illegal acts committed against them. The only difference, however, is that being black is not illegal in the eyes of the law, even though many blacks are treated as though it were. Homosexuals' extra-legal status brings a different dimension to our situation, to our necessity for political action. The whole concept of "working within the system" for change is thrown out of kilter, because we do not have legal status in that system. However, homosexuals who have studied other movements that have resorted to trying to "break" the system and that have gone the guns and bombs route know that this tactic ends in the *literal* destruction of the group. The prime example of this is the Panthers who were methodically murdered by "law enforcement officers."

There is no one group that has a large enough power base to accomplish its goal of changing the system. To believe anything to the contrary is unrealistic. Power, i.e., financial, political, and military power and their implied threat of violence to those who resist it, is not and never has been available to any oppressed group. It is therefore fallacious to assume that an oppressed minority can speak of "power" in that sense of the word. Any minority group which has tried to use power (control by violence) has learned that power is not only unavailable as a method but is, as practiced by the oppressor, unavoidable by the oppressed group.

131

There is no effective way for minorities, as they are now functioning within their separate movements, to achieve the degree of power necessary for effecting any major change in their condition.

The law-keeping forces are aware of this fact; that is why they are kept so busy harassing organizations which shift from social to political activity. It is why the harassment is increased when organizations begin to work together.

When D.O.B. began to transform from a social gathering-place into a politically active organization, it became the target of intensified harassment, especially when it organized activity in conjunction with other groups. One of the organizations with which we began to work regularly was the Gay Activists Alliance, which has to date been the most active in attempting to effect changes in oppressive and discriminatory legislation. Its members have been brutalized on more occasions than there is room here to list; however, I would like to cite a few incidents as described in the February 1972 *Gay Activist* (GAA's newsletter):

GAY CLUBBED AT MUSKIE RALLY

. . . The demonstration began at 7:00 P.M. with a picket line, posters, flyers and chants. Senator Muskie is one of the few acknowledged candidates who has [sic] refused to take a stand on gay rights. . . . The only incident that occurred before Muskie's arrival was a request by the police that we move our picket line 40 feet down the block (in front of an alley way) where we were told "we could still be heard." Knowing that we had every right to demonstrate where we stood, we refused. . . . Then it happened. Without any provocation police began shoving Gays from behind and one, Patrolman Sicignano (Badge No. 26496) of the 19th Precinct suddenly lunged at Gay activist Charlie Brown, kicked him in the groin, knocked him to the ground and then

132

proceeded pounding him brutally across his head with a billy club. Charlie lay unconscious. Another cop was overheard telling Sicignano, "You beat him up, now you'll have to arrest him." Charlie was dragged off. The demonstration dispersed. . . . Back at the Police Station, Charlie later told us Sicignano was asking his fellow patrolmen what he should book Charlie for. They decided to charge him with "harassment," presumably for placing his head in the arc of a swinging billy club. Charlie was later released on a Vera Summons. . . . When we arrived at the Precinct Charlie's head was still bleeding well after an hour after the beating. "Why didn't you treat his wound?" we asked. "What wound?" one cop answered. "I hope he bleeds to death," another said. We took Charlie to the hospital where he was X-rayed and his head was shaven and stitched. . . .

Another example, from the same issue of the GAA newsletter, points up the sadism involved:

SUFFOLK VIOLENCE CONTINUES

In the latest of a seeming endless series of beatings of Gays in Suffolk County, two GAA members were attacked and beaten by two "assailants" on December 21 on their way to present testimony at the District Attorney's office in Riverhead.

The current series began when the Corral Bar at Hollbrook was "raided"—the owner, bartenders and many customers clubbed, beaten and then arrested—on November 20.

The arresting officers were two plainclothesmen who had been drinking heavily (the bartender's tally showed 15 drinks between them at the Corral) and molesting patrons. They left the bar shortly to return with additional police officers and declared a raid. The raid was carried out "Suffolk Style" with attendant clubbings and punching of faces.

On December 14, L.I. and N.Y. GAA held a demonstra-

133

tion protesting the November 20 assaults at the Corral. In the course of the protest several demonstrators including Cora Perrota, Sylvia Rivera and Charles Burch were arrested, insulted and roughed up. Charles Burch who had been beaten up and arrested in the August 22nd Hauppage demonstration (see September *Gay Activist*) was on this occasion left alone in a cell with its door unlocked. Two men entered the cell, identified themselves as the officers—Lewis Gentles and Peter Goegehegan—who had initiated the Corral raid. They beat Charlie, threatened his life, and warned "the next time you're arrested, we'll make sure there is a gun on you. . . ."

The United States government in collusion with the police and the courts undermines movement organizations, in fact denies civil rights to citizens within these organizations by this method of arbitrarily and illegally converting citizens into "criminals" who are in turn jailed. Such citizens are political prisoners of the state. The Attica prison uprising was organized and carried out in good part by political prisoners . . . We all know how that ended.

When I speak on college campuses, inevitably one of the students will say, "What about the good cops? You can't say that all cops are bad." My answer is that all members of police departments do exactly what they are told to do, without any question. They are not encouraged or for that matter allowed to think about or analyze the orders they are given, any more than are members of the military. A cop who saves a drowning child one day may well be out beating the heads of minority members the next day, because he is "following orders." In an oppressive society labels are attached to various segments of the population—"black mili-

134

tants," "campus radicals," "anti-war demonstrators," "gay activists," and so on. When the order is given to move in on those so labeled and to remove their civil rights by illegal police actions, *every* cop obeys. If he doesn't, he is not a cop for long. The good cops, those who question the system as did Frank Serpico, are misfits in police departments, which are used against segments of the citizenry they are purported to protect. As long as our corrupt and oppressive society continues in fragmentation under a corrupt and oppressive government, we cannot expect to encounter a good cop.

It should be observed that GAA and D.O.B. had in the past turned to all of the proper authorities with their grievances, including police precincts and the mayor's office. GAA has given complete reports on a number of their members' illegal arrests and brutalization to councilmen, assemblymen, congressmen, the mayor, and the governor, among others. *Nothing comes of it.* In fact, not only has lack of action been manifest; so has the lack of *intent* to act, as was demonstrated during a meeting at the mayor's office which GAA and D.O.B. set up to protest police harassment. We met with Barry Godderer and several other persons on the mayor's staff, outlined our grievances, and explored what might be done to alleviate harassment. After listening to my account of the D.O.B. harassment, Godderer said, "Oh, well, maybe it isn't so bad—maybe they just came around for a payoff." In other words, maybe they were "good cops" just looking to get their pockets lined with what is euphemistically called "protection money." What is appalling is that this motive seemed acceptable to Mr. Godderer!

At another point in our discussion we explained that homosexual organizations and their meeting places are extremely important in so far as they provide a place where

135

homosexuals can meet, other than gay bars which so often have been raided at random and which usually press high-priced, watered-down drinks in rapid order on unwilling customers. At this point Godderer said, "You know, that's really hard to understand, you'd think the cops would be *for* places like that—after all, it gets *them* off the streets" (my italics). Basically the meeting was a farce, and other meetings like it have so often been tinged with either overt or submerged hostilities and prejudices, or with an attitude of placating in order to eliminate the "nuisance value" of protesting minority groups. Ultimately nothing is done to right the wrongs and social injustices.

Police have a seemingly bland method of beginning violence at an otherwise peaceful demonstration: asking demonstrators to move from the site of their demonstration. When a group refuses to move there is always the threat of police brutality and the possibility of arrests. One instance, which did end in illegal arrests, took place on October 23, 1972, during a peaceful "Women Against Richard Nixon" (W.A.R.N.) demonstration in front of the Nixon campaign headquarters on Madison Avenue in New York. Ti-Grace Atkinson, Florynce Kennedy, Ellen Povill, Merle Goldberg, and I were arrested.

Flo Kennedy is a lawyer, and we had two additional attorneys at the station within half an hour of our arrest, so we received less brutalizing and high-handed treatment than most who are arrested. One of our attorneys was thrown to the floor and arrested because she refused to leave the precinct before her clients were issued their Vera Summonses. As far as we know, the request to leave a precinct before clients are released has never been made to any other

136

lawyer. Male attorneys who know about the case, including Leonard Boudin, who appeared in court on our lawyer's behalf, agree that this would never have happened to a male lawyer—they were appalled.

The usual "strip and squat" vaginal search of women prisoners was not carried out on us, despite an approach to me by a woman cop to "unzip your pants," and to Ellen to "lift your skirt." Most women are subjected to this dehumanizing assault against their persons when they have been arrested. Ellen told me later that when she asked why she should lift her skirt, the woman replied, "To search for contraband."

We were fortunate enough to have movement lawyers handle our case without charge. Most of the poor, who cannot gain access to the limited time of the few movement lawyers available to handle such cases, are often given inadequate legal advice, or are incarcerated in jails, where they languish as non-persons because there is no one to look after their legal needs.

Merle Goldberg was arrested at the demonstration for "disorderly conduct" because she asked one of the cops, a lieutenant, for his badge number, which he had covered with tape—this is often done when cops move in on a demonstration. Merle asked for his badge number—a totally legitimate request—because he had a stranglehold around Ti-Grace's throat and was pulling her head backward by her hair. I was thrown bodily into the police van by two cops; when I got up, I saw the lieutenant and two other cops dragging Ti-Grace to the door of the van. One of them yelled, "Get this fucking bitch in there." The lieutenant, who still had his arm around her throat, reached his other arm over her head and slid his fingers under her glasses. I yelled "Stop that," and struck at his arm. Applying pressure to the eyes is a police tactic familiar to a number of people who have been arrested.

This encounter with the cops, no matter how unpleasant, was a mild one. However, our police records remain despite the fact that all charges against us were dropped, and the arrests will continue to stand against our names.

What is perhaps most frightening about all this is that the data processing of records and dossiers, the increased invasion of privacy, the interchange of information among agencies, including F.B.I., C.I.A., police departments, credit bureaus, and employment agencies, are fast encroaching on our constitutional rights.

In his article "Marked for Life—Have You Ever Been Arrested?" in the April 13, 1974, issue of *The New York Times Magazine,* Aryeh Neier points out that "The F.B.I. is the major source of arrest-record information. As a matter of routine, almost all police departments in the country forward to the bureau for filing the fingerprints of persons they have arrested . . . a bureau official reported that, on the average working day, the bureau received 29,000 sets of fingerprints. Only 13,000 came from law-enforcement agencies. The remaining 16,000 sets were sent in by banks, insurance companies, government employers (municipal, county, state, and federal), licensing agencies, and the like. In return, these agencies received from the F.B.I. whatever information it had in its files on the 29,000 persons involved."

It must be kept in mind that the information given and taken indicates records of *arrest*—there is no indication of the *disposal* of the arrest whether there was a conviction, an acquittal, or whether the charges were dismissed. Many

138

people have lost jobs, been harassed, and had their lives disrupted because of this unjust system, which is maintained, not as it is touted, to "protect the public," but rather to protect the corporate image from "undesirables."

Other more formalized methods of intruding into the private lives of people applying for jobs, housing, or credit include checks into police records of arrests, direct questioning methods, and lie-detector tests.

D.O.B. and GAA members entered the offices of Fidelifacts of Greater New York, founded by Vincent Gillen (a former F.B.I. agent). Fidelifacts is one of the several investigatory agencies used by big businesses. Many companies will not hire or will fire anybody who is found to be homosexual or who evidences "homosexual tendencies." John Cye Cheastey (a former Secret Service, Internal Revenue, and Navy Intelligence man) is now an investigator for Fidelifacts and points out, ". . . more and more companies are making 'extensive pre-employment checkups' before hiring such people applying for managerial positions. . . . I think that industrial intelligence is one of the fastest growing businesses in the United States today. . . ." A few years ago in a speech to the Association of Stock Exchange Brokers, Vincent Gillen said that "establishing that someone is a homosexual is often difficult, but I like to go on the rule of thumb that if one looks like a duck, walks like a duck, associates only with ducks, and quacks like a duck, he is probably a duck."

D.O.B. and GAA members entered the offices of Fidelifacts while other of our members picketed on the street. One demonstrator was wearing a marvelous duck costume to attract the attention of passersby in the hope that they would read the leaflets we were passing out.

139

Those of us who went into the offices (including members of the press and a television camera crew) were told that Gillen was out of town. A couple of Fidelifacts men started shoving one of our members who had demanded to see Gillen. Ultimately the police were called. They arrived in force; this was covered by the television camera crew. We were told to leave the offices or face arrests. Since arrests would have resulted in a lot of police harassment, and since we believed that the purpose of our demonstration against invasion of privacy would be well covered by the media, we left the offices.

That night on the television news coverage of the event Vincent Gillen appeared and explained that his agency did not discriminate against any group, that he served an important function in the community. No editorial comment was made on the insidious aspect of his agency's work and of others like it around the country. The threat to privacy— all peoples' privacy—was totally glossed over. The event was covered as another one of those funny gay demonstrations that "we seem to be seeing more and more of."

Mr. Neier reports in his *Arrest* article that:

> Each year, law-enforcement agencies grow more efficient in disseminating records. The Bureau's [F.B.I.] Identification Division, which was receiving 29,000 sets of fingerprints daily in 1970, is only a manual system operating through the U.S. mail. Recently, to supplement this service, the bureau established a computerized system, the National Crime Information Center, to speed the exchange of records with local law-enforcement agencies around the country. Private industry is in the record-keeping and record-selling business in a big way. The biggest firm in the business, Retail Credit Company of Atlanta, has more than 7,000 employees, maintains dossiers on about 45 million people and produces more

than 35 million reports a year. The member firms of a trade association known as the Associated Credit Bureau, which among them do a business of close to $1 billion a year, maintain files on about 110 million Americans.

The information in these files is sold to creditors, employers, and landlords. In other words, they are making money, in part, on the records of illegal arrests. Much of the information sold by the credit bureaus comes from the files of police departments.

A position paper on "Employment Discrimination against Homosexuals" which GAA prepared and presented to the New York City Commission on Human Rights early in 1971 includes the following:

ANTI-HOMOSEXUAL PRACTICES: UNIVERSAL THREAT TO PRIVACY

Nobody is immune to the threat of anti-homosexual practices as long as they are legal—these practices may be used against any person, regardless of sexual orientation, at any time and in some cases without his knowledge.

Credit bureau checkup reports . . . are never seen by the person investigated. Oftimes, reports of "homosexual behavior" or "homosexual tendencies" are based on hearsay or on other flimsy circumstantial evidence. Sources of "evidence" can range anywhere from what Gillen refers to in his "duck" analogy to the possession of a nude David [statue] in one's house or the receiving of a gay publication in the mail. [Note: the Gay Activists Alliance was considering furnishing complimentary subscriptions for *Gay* and the *Los Angeles Advocate* to members of the New York City Commission on Human Rights, in order to keep them abreast of developments. However, after further consideration, the GAA decided not to follow through on this gesture on the

141

grounds that it would subject members of the Commission to possible loss of their insurance and possible inclusion of this "derogatory" information in their checkup reports—which they are not permitted to review or see. GAA sincerely hopes that its concern for the Commission members is reciprocated through a show of concern by Commission members for the human rights of homosexuals facing this very kind of harassment every day.]

Allstate Insurance Company, which bases much of its information on this kind of circumstantial "evidence" "not only denies or cancels the insurance [if they turn up any "evidence" of homosexuality] but files a copy of the report with the police, the credit bureau, the employer and the insurance bureau. . . ."

The very fact that these investigations are an intrusion into the private lives of all people, despite their sexual orientation, is further reason to condemn the anti-homosexual witch hunt. . . . In Federal employment, Internal Revenue Service employees found to have had any association whatever with a homosexual, are subject to dismissal regardless of the sexual orientation of the employee [only social association need be proven for dismissal, not sexual relationship]. In short, the end result of the witch hunt is that millions of homosexual employees, as well as millions of heterosexual employees, are subject to dismissal on the basis of hearsay evidence, evidence based on friendship associations, evidence based on what one might receive in the mail [since investigations often involve the interrogation of an individual's *mailman!*], evidence based on personal charges made by an enemy of an individual—all sorts of circumstantial evidence pointing to an individual's sexual orientation. Gillen [head man of Fidelifacts] defended the collection and distribution of this kind of information by stating his opinion that homosexuals, though they are "usually good workers with above average intelligence . . . could take advantage of their employers' finances." *Could* take

advantage . . . ! Circumstantial evidence to prevent the
hiring of an individual for a crime never committed!

Several years ago the pay telephone at the Gay Community Center was bugged. If there had ever been any doubt
on the matter it was dispelled when one of the people at
the center put in a dime one day to make a call. He said,
covering the mouthpiece, "Hey, come and listen to this!"
In turn, a number of us listened. By some electronic quirk,
the bug had gotten reversed and we were receiving police
calls over the Center's telephone!

About two years ago Ellen and I were talking on the telephone; she was in her office and I was at our home. The
conversation ended like this:

RUTH: Goodbye, hon, and I love you.

ELLEN: I love you and . . .

MAN'S VOICE: And I love you.

The surveillance of politically active homosexuals is common and often the procedures are quite involved: I have a
small cabin on four acres of woodland in upstate New York.
For the more than eleven years that I've had the place, I
have listed my telephone there in the local directory under
R. Simpson. That listing has never changed, and Ellen has
never had her name listed in the directory; nor has she had
a listing in New York City where we live. Her business
(which does not include her name) is listed in the New
York City directory. A couple of months ago she received a
telephone call at her business office and a woman asked her,
"Is Ruth there?" When Ellen asked who was calling, the
woman answered, "This is the telephone company in
Poughkeepsie. Is this Ellen?" Needless to say, Ellen was
astonished and asked the telephone representative how she
had gotten her (Ellen's) business number. The woman said

143

that she "didn't know." Ellen told her she would have me call her, and called me at home with the story. Immediately I called the upstate telephone office and demanded to know how they knew Ellen's name and her business telephone number in the city, and knew that there was any connection between us. The representative fumbled and stuttered, asked me to hold on, and went through a ridiculous set of "guesses" as to how she might possibly have gotten the number, including suggesting that I "might have given it to the telephone company so that I could be reached in New York City." When I said that this never happened and that, furthermore, her company had my home telephone number in the city, she asked me to hold on again. When she returned, she said in her best "Lily Tomlin" telephone voice, "I can not at this time tell you how the number happens to appear on your record at this office. I can only say that it is the result of an investigatory process."

Minority members should be alerted to the fact that the Big Brother government plan predicted by George Orwell in his book *1984* may have a premature birth. Representative William Moorhead made public a secret White House study of a government communications network proposed for every home radio and television set and boat and automobile radio. Moorhead said that his staff investigators had learned that two alternative plans to link the government with private homes through electronic devices have already been tested. One of the systems uses AM radio waves and the other uses a device operating through television networks and home receivers. A couple of engineers have told me that by making a reasonably simple electronic adjustment in the cable TV system a two-way, *sender-receiver* system can easily be established. (It is interesting to note that Representative Moorhead announced he would conduct open hearings on

144

the White House study in 1973; however, to my knowledge, this was never done.)

Not only are we and our organizations bugged, harassed, and generally treated in the most humiliating fashion, but our organizations are infiltrated by agents. In the homosexual movement, as in all movements, there are many who are just naturally destructive, counter-revolutionary, and generally damaging to that movement. Actually, the infiltration of agents is not necessary to the degree in which this method is used, since there are so many "unpaid agents," people who consider themselves in the movement and who go around doing destructive things which ultimately are instrumental in either downgrading or destroying an organization. But then, we have learned from Watergate and its aftermath that high-placed government agencies are often avid advocates of overkill—better safe than sorry, they seem to figure, so let's infiltrate and sabotage, just to be doubly sure.

The use of paid agents provocateurs against the homosexual movement is common. In one instance such agents were used in an attempt to destroy the public image of GAA at the end of April 1973. For the third time in three years a bill, called the "gay rights" bill, to end discrimination in employment, housing, and public accommodations was defeated by the New York City Council at the end of April. It was defeated by one vote—requiring eight "yes" votes to pass, it received only seven, the closest vote on the bill to that time. Yet Councilman Thomas Manton (who abstained from voting) and Councilwoman Aileen Ryan (who was absent from the vote) had both promised, orally and in writing, to vote "yes" on the bill. This would of course have meant that the bill would have passed. Before and while the vote was being taken, about one hundred GAA people demonstrated

145

peacefully outside City Hall. When the bill's defeat was announced to the demonstrators, about seventy-five of them went to the ramp of the Brooklyn Bridge and in protest lay down across the roadway. Fifteen men and five women, including officers and executive board members of GAA, were arrested.

The following day Councilwoman Ryan announced that during the previous night she had received about forty telephone calls at her home and that a number of times during these calls her life had been threatened. She described the calls as abusive, vulgar, frightening. She asked for police protection and said that she had to be away from the voting session "to make a speech," but that "if I had been there to vote, I certainly would have voted 'no,' and obviously that vote would have been justified." Mrs. Ryan spoke of the horror of the calls and reported that she was informed that they (the callers) had "formed a corporation for Aileen is dead, dead, dead." She went on to say that the callers, in the manner of a news broadcast, announced that "Councilwoman Ryan has just been found dead, having been strangled. She was found with a jock strap around her neck." She related that the callers told her "they would cut off personal parts of my anatomy." She expressed the opinion that she had been singled out because "I am a woman." Her son, who was with her at the press conference, held a scarecrow-type effigy which had been placed in front of the door of her home. It had a "bloody" head and was decorated with a cross.

(It is necessary to know that GAA functions on the premise of nonviolence. I know and have worked with many of the people who are currently officers and members, and know from past demonstrations and political actions that GAA has never violated its code of nonviolence. Through creative planning and hard work by its officers and members, it has always been able to make its impact felt without resorting to violence or threats of violence.)

At about 5 P.M. on April 28 I talked to Bruce Voeller, then GAA's president, who said that of course nobody from GAA had made the calls, that he and others in the group were arranging for interviews with the media to refute any connection between the calls and GAA; he said that he had been interviewed by CBS-TV and that Ron Gold (GAA media coordinator) was to be interviewed by Channel 5. Other interviews with Channels 7 and 11 and with *The New York Times* were to be conducted.

I listened to the CBS-TV 6 P.M. news. There was a lengthy statement by Mrs. Ryan, described above, and a very brief statement, obviously edited from a taped interview with Bruce, which included nothing he might have said about disassociating GAA from the calls. The only part of Bruce's statement that was used concerned his comments on Mrs. Ryan's harassment, which, he said, was precisely what the bill was all about. He said that about a million homosexuals in New York City are harassed daily. The implication of the segment of the interview which the network chose to telecast was certainly not at all a positive GAA refutation of the calls and the import of their violence. Anyone who did not know GAA and its people might well have assumed that the calls had indeed been made by GAA members.

On Channel 7's 7 P.M. news there was another interview with Mrs. Ryan which again included her lengthy comments on the calls. At the end of the interview, the newscaster said that he had "received a call from a GAA representative who said that GAA is nonviolent and that GAA believed that those councilmen who were not on hand to vote on the bill had been offered political favors for being absent." The basic intent of the GAA message was glossed over in this third-person treatment.

I listened to CBS radio past the 9 P.M. news cycle, and although Mrs. Ryan's statement was given twice, there was no statement of any sort from GAA. At 10 P.M., the local station, Channel 5, finally presented an interview which got to the heart of the issue. Since it was live, Bruce was able to make a total and untampered-with statement.

It was not until the next evening that NBC-TV network news presented live interviews with Bruce Voeller and Ginny Vida (then vice-president of GAA) which not only presented GAA's policy of nonviolence and its firm opposition to threats of violence, but also exposed highly questionable political tactics, including "arm-twisting," by Council majority leader Thomas J. Cuite. And finally in the interview the harassment charge against GAA was thrown back into the lap of Cuite when Bruce said that "GAA, at this point, is not at all sure if the calls to and harassment of Mrs. Ryan had not been promoted by Cuite, who is well known for his strong-arm political tactics."

In an article in the May 1973 issue of *Majority Report,* a feminist newspaper, Ginny Vida wrote: "Realizing that his vote in support of Intro 475 [the number of the homosexual rights bill] was vital to its passage . . . New York City Councilman Manton asked to have a proxy vote accepted, since he planned to be out of town on the day of the voting. Cuite, an open opponent of the bill, refused to approve the proxy. Manton then drove all the way from Pennsylvania to cast his vote in person, only to confront his elderly father, who had been brought to City Hall from Queens. Manton senior told his son that if he voted 'yes' on the bill he would never speak to him again. Manton came back to the council meeting visibly shaken and with tears in his eyes. Councilman Manton abstained, withholding the single approval necessary for the passage of the bill."

In the spring of 1974 the bill, this time labeled Intro 2, was defeated by a vote of 22 to 19. In early 1975 the bill (Intro 54) lay dormant, with little prospect of its being voted out of committee in the near future.

Homosexuals are illegal, simply by *being;* however, the laws against us are not equally enforced because: we cannot be easily classified; if we are identified, often we are not pursued by law enforcement agencies; we are mildly harassed if we meet in a purely social setting; those of us who become politically active are more severely harassed; if we attempt to work with other groups or other movements, we face probable arrest and possible imprisonment. Corrupt laws are used to discourage us from organizing in a political sense. And when we do organize, law enforcement agencies are used against us, as they are against political segments of all minority groups, to deter our uniquely precarious progress toward full citizenship.

149

9

The Homosexual Movement
One Forward Step
–Then Two Steps Back

Daughters of Bilitis,* founded in 1955 in San Francisco, was the first lesbian organization formed in the United States. Over the next decade and a half, chapters were organized in a few other major cities, including New York. D.O.B., New York, got its Certificate of Authority from the Department of State on October 27, 1969, although it had been in existence for about six years prior to that time.

Until 1969 D.O.B., New York, functioned as a social-educational organization. During that year the Radicalesbians was formed; women also functioned within the male-dominated structures of Gay Liberation Front, West Side Discussion Group, and Gay Activists Alliance. Mattachine had only one woman active in its leadership at the time.

Today, D.O.B., New York, is gone, along with some of its

---

* This name comes from a collection of lesbian love poems by Pierre Louÿs, *The Songs of Bilitis.*

sister chapters. Similarly, other homosexual organizations have passed from the scene and new ones have sprung up. In the last couple of years the Lesbian Feminist Liberation organization was formed by GAA women who broke off from that organization in order to create an all-woman group. The National Gay Task Force is a homosexual organization in which both men and women work together. There are a few women still involved in GAA itself.

The organizations in the homosexual movement often come and go, grow strong and then weaken, as they develop visibility and political orientation. This is true of most minority group organizations. To believe that this pattern is accidental is naive. As president of D.O.B. I experienced its disintegration; I have also seen other organizations in the homosexual movement, and in other minority movements, dissolve in similar fashion. Though issues may differ, the disruption and demise of groups follow the old familiar pattern.

The presidency of D.O.B. came to me by default in 1970. I had been active as education and program director, had been doing a good deal of the general work, and was on the governing board. When the presidency and vice-presidency became vacant, the board decided that I should be appointed acting president until elections. Quite rightly, it felt that nobody else would want the presidency, because of the perils and problems that went with the post. Prior to the elections, I asked if just one more woman wouldn't like to place her name on the slate. It worried me that mine was the only name on the ballot.

Another thing had been worrying me: the national convention of D.O.B. chapters held in the summer of 1970 voted to make each chapter autonomous. Previously each chapter had had to report to and receive approval from the

151

national office. Our D.O.B. constitution and by-laws, which had until this time functioned well for many years, required a few minor changes to reflect this new chapter autonomy. At a board meeting following the convention, I brought up the by-laws for discussion, saying that these necessary though minor changes should be made and that when they were approved, multiple copies should be made and provided to each dues-paying member. This had never been done before. By rights, a by-laws committee should have been appointed; however, there were no women available or willing to form such a committee, so the board decided that, since I was familiar with such matters, I should draft the required changes. I did so, and they were approved by the board.

A short while later, we found quarters of our own, a loft on Prince Street in the downtown Soho area of New York City. We worked literally day and night getting the loft ready. We built our own partitions for office, library, and kitchen space, secured fireproof material for curtains, painted, had some plumbing and electrical work done. We were also fighting court battles, dealing with police harassment, working on political actions with GAA and on our own; we were arranging new programs, action meetings; we were trying to get incorporation under a New York State charter (the organization was chartered under the West Coast parent D.O.B., and since we were autonomous we wanted to get our own New York State charter, a long and involved legal process); we were also working on getting a certificate of occupancy, and in this connection had a meeting with the fire marshal, who inspected the center and told us while at that time no tenants of lofts in the Soho area were being given occupancy signs, as long as we kept the place as clean as it was we would have no trouble. The few

152

women doing most of the work also held full-time jobs, and often contributed their own money to D.O.B. when funds ran short. Such was the state of the organization before the center was officially opened and functioning.

We opened the center early in January 1971 and it was going strong. Very strong. We had excellent attendance, and gradually the organization became well known for its political actions, educational programs, and parties—there was something for everybody. We put out a monthly newsletter; we had gotten a jukebox; we decorated the center for each dance; we provided refreshments and hauled beer and soda from a wholesale supplier; we kept the place and its facilities clean and pleasant. But still only a very few were willing to do the work. Anyone who has been involved in an organization knows that while only a handful do the work the other members often become vocal about complaints. "How come you don't have chocolate doughnuts this week?" "Can't you get the kind of cups that the wax doesn't come off the rim?" "Why don't you have the really new records on the jukebox?" "Why do we have to have all this new stuff—can't we have some softer, slower music?" And one week, when we couldn't find white toilet paper at the market: "Doesn't D.O.B. care about ecology? Why don't you get white paper?" But these are all low-level complaints from the quiet complainers, and represent "family" discontent—the kind that can be exploited by outside disrupters.

What are some of the early symptoms? When a structured organization finds itself spending a lot of time discussing whether the chairs should be arranged in a circle or not; whether "homosexual" isn't really a "sexist" word, so why don't we call ourselves "dykes"; whether non-members shouldn't be allowed to vote on administrative and other issues in order to avoid an "elitist" structure—that organization is about to be undermined by those who level the charges. When time and energy are wasted discussing with the pseudo-militants whether members of the group should or should not be interviewed by the "pig, capitalistic press," and when these same "militants" start meeting with other members outside the organization—often with the ultra-conservative faction which believes the group is moving too fast politically—watch out!

All of this happened at D.O.B. Some specific complaints from these "militants" strangely had to do with very "establishment" issues: charges that D.O.B. had no by-laws—it did; that D.O.B. had no charter—it did; that D.O.B. had no occupancy sign—it didn't and wasn't about to get one at the time; that D.O.B. faced the possibility of losing its home—it did, since the landlord had talked of future plans to turn the building into a co-op.*

How the disrupters used Roberts Rules of Order is so classic it bears attention: following our May 1971 D.O.B. Open Discussion, which on the night in question was neither "open" nor a "discussion," the following floor plan for disruption was subsequently found by two board members who were cleaning up the center. Obviously, the two crumpled pieces of paper were not meant for our attention; the "master plan" had been photocopied prior to the meeting —what we found was a photocopy—and handed out to various members intent on disrupting the proceedings.

The chart that follows, then, is a reproduction, not of the meeting as it happened but the plan for disruption as drawn up in advance. As the reader will see, it proposes various

---

* This last was a battle we would have fought and won, doubtless with a large enough settlement to acquire a new "home." We had fought issues more difficult in the past. The only battle we couldn't win was the one with our "sisters."

alternatives, based on the things that I might do or say (it should be noted, however, that at no time in D.O.B.'s history had anyone suggested that meetings be taped). Confusing as the chart may seem, its intent is clear: to sow chaos and fear, and turn the meeting into a shambles:

Ruth starts to speak.

Question: Is the meeting called to order?

Ruth: There aren't enough people here yet.	Ruth continues talking.	
		Ruth calls meeting to order.
Group does other things so R. can't speak until meeting is called to order.		
	R. does not stipulate Roberts Rules.	R. stipulates Roberts Rules
	Someone suggests it.	
R. turns on tape recorder.	R. suggests recording the discussion.	R. does *not* say anything about recording.
Point of Personal Privilege: would be hurt if women would leave because of the recorder; if a single person objects, there must not be taping.		She does grant it.
She doesn't grant it.		SHOW OF HANDS OF OBJECTORS

[*Continued*]

155

[*Continued from previous page*]

Motion: No taping if anyone objects.

NO TAPING

SECOND THE MOTION

This Issue May Arise At Any Time.

DISCUSSION

Ruth: Only members can vote.

VOTE

Point of Personal Privilege: R. included people in the Newsletter who are not members and since this an open discussion, I don't think that non-members should be discriminated against.

GRANTED

REFUSED

MOTION: EVERYONE PRESENT MAY VOTE TONIGHT

VOTE

SECOND

DISCUSSION

VOTE

MOTION CARRIED

MOTION DEFEATED

Point of personal privilege: (same as above—keep repeating again and again, if necessary).

156

Ruth opens her mouth.

Point of Information: There is a paper which has been prepared by several people that directly covers issues of the Newsletter. The paper ought to be read now and in its entirety and without interruption.

DENIED

GRANTED: IT CAN BE
READ, ETC.

Point of Personal Privilege: I was mentioned. I was grievously injured by the Newsletter and it must be read now.

GRANTED   DENIED

Who has it?

A. rises with it: I have it and there will be copies, for everyone [passed around].

A. starts to read.

INTERRUPTIONS

From floor:
Out of order.

READ TO END
WITHOUT
INTERRUPTION

[Continued]

157

[Continued from previous page]

Motion to remove
heckler.

SECOND

DISCUSSION

MOTION CARRIED

When I showed a leader in the black movement the floor plan, she said: "Why, that's right out of an agent's handbook!" As background, some of the "get-the-guns militants" had been meeting outside D.O.B. with some of the conservatives who thought D.O.B. was "too political." These illassorted groups were working together on the night of the Open Discussion. Here was a conglomeration of women with totally disparate attitudes and, for once, they were acting *in concert*. It would have been impossible to get both groups to act collectively at a demonstration (militant), or at decorating the center (non-political), or drafting by-laws (administrative); for disruption, however, they were willing to join ranks.

There had been rumors of a takeover of D.O.B.—some said it would be from the "left." I doubted that, since at the time there was no more politically active lesbian organization anywhere. Others said the takeover would be from the "right," which I tended to believe, since this is the route usually taken by many political organizations which show symptoms of advanced disruption. Also, I knew the women involved: they were either ultra-conservative or "pseudomilitants."

In any case, the two papers mentioned in the floor plan were read, and I was finally allowed to give a very brief report, punctuated by loud interruptions, on a meeting at the mayor's office, the final meeting with the fire marshal,

158

the status of the charter, a membership vote on the amended by-laws, the most recent cop harassment, and the fact that the board had voted to buy an inexpensive tape recorder and camera in order to document future harassment at the Center. But no one really cared.

The members were not willing to do the work, whether of a social or political nature. Therefore, they had no understanding of the issues involved, no knowledge that they were being exploited by the disrupters.

That night in May 1971 ended in violence, with chairs being knocked over, when I said that I would no longer participate in the discussion and walked out with a few officers and board members who were also present.

The following week I and the rest of the board resigned. What happened ultimately to D.O.B. represents a classic example of how a movement organization is disrupted and destroyed; how the disrupters themselves learn that there aren't as many doers, i.e., "leaders," "elitists," "superstars" (all of which I was called), as they had imagined; how the disrupters themselves are forced to become doers and then end up as the "elitists" in the next cycle of disruption.

Ultimately, as I had predicted, the takeover was from the right. In the few remaining months of D.O.B.'s life the following events occurred:

• It was announced in a subsequent Newsletter that D.O.B. had held a meeting with the local precinct and was "working with the officers" toward solving some of the problems. D.O.B. also announced that it could no longer work with GAA because of the chauvinistic attitudes of the men. The women were willing to meet with cops, but were unwilling to work with their oppressed brothers. (Hardly a revolutionary development!)

• The August Newsletter reported that "a list of eleven

159

defaults was delivered to D.O.B. A few of our most serious defaults were: placing advertising which ruined the reputation of the building . . ." D.O.B. actually stopped advertising its meetings in the *Village Voice* as a result. Few things represent greater oppression than the denial of the right to advertise. That those running a lesbian organization would accede to such a denial, and, further, regard that right as "a serious default," is clearly counter-revolutionary.

• The calendar of events in the September Newsletter represented a poor joke on those "super-militants" who argued that D.O.B. was not militant enough to suit them. It did not include one action meeting, educational presentation, or workshop—all of these had been supplanted by a string of dances.

Toward the end, D.O.B. was meeting in a church. I was invited to speak, and went. I tried to give the women some background on movement fragmentation, as well as some suggestions for what might still be done to save D.O.B. Following the meeting, a couple of the women who had been trying to hold D.O.B. together asked me to return—they found that the major problems were "getting women to work or take responsibility" and "trying to keep others from their constant disruptions."

Shortly after this meeting, D.O.B., New York, ceased functioning.

To believe that the dissolution of D.O.B. and of many other non-"establishment" organizations is caused exclusively by people who are ill-advised and unintentionally disruptive is a serious error. D.O.B., we know, was infiltrated by at least two government agents.

Basically there are two types of agents: First, the provocateur/informer: this type sometimes leads the group, or some of its members, into actions which can easily be documented as illegal and which are in some instances politically suicidal. This kind of agent is militant (i.e. "pseudo-militant") and active in the organization's political actions.

The second is the "quiet type" who joins the group, blends in as one of the ranks, informs on the group's activities, and turns in the names of those active in the group.

One example of the provocateur/informer is given in *The New York Times* May 20, 1973, news story headed: "F.B.I. Informer Is Linked to Bombings and Protests by Weathermen Groups." The article begins: "One of the most militant and out-spoken members of the radical Weathermen organization during its peak period of bombing and other violence in late 1969 and early 1970 was an informer and agent provocateur for the Federal Bureau of Investigation, private Government sources said today." The sources said further that the informer, Larry D. Grathwohl of Cincinnati, Ohio, had acknowledged participating in bombings and violent demonstrations while living in various underground Weathermen collectives around the country. In 1970 the sources said Mr. Grathwohl was often in direct contact with Guy L. Goodwin, the chief Justice Department official who was prosecuting criminal cases against the Weathermen. Such contact between an informer and a prosecutor is against the department's regulations.

A former Weatherman, Robert Burlingham, who managed *Ramparts* magazine, described the agent in this way:

> Larry was absolutely a provocateur. I can remember one meeting in Cincinnati where there was a discussion going on about the question of armed political resistance and the various bombings that had occurred. Grathwohl

161

took the initiative as was his wont and began castigating people for talking about the destruction of property; he said it wasn't enough to carry on these kinds of bombings. "True revolutionaries," he said, "had to be ready and anxious to kill people."

A Congressional source reported in the article that he had been told privately of the agent's activities and added that F.B.I. officials described the agent as a "straight guy who does what he's told." It was only after Grathwohl supplied information that led to the arrests in New York of two members of the Weathermen (Linda Evans and Dianne Donghi, and we'll let the term Weather*men* ride) that he was suspected by the Weathermen of being an informer.

This kind of agent is extremely difficult to detect; but it is possible. One of the women who is undoubtedly an informer-agent in the homosexual movement has always been on hand at debacles which have led to the disruption and dissolution of homosexual organizations—she was there at the Gay Community Center, Gay Liberation Front, D.O.B., and she advocates "getting guns" and "breaking the system," and uses other pseudo-militant rhetoric. She also was present at the politically suicidal women's "takeover" of the 5th Street House in New York City. It was shortly after this that the squatters' movement disappeared.

On April 5, 1971, GAA sent out "An Appeal to All Gay Groups and Newspapers from the Gay Activists Alliance of New York." It delineated a series of disruptions which had occurred at a national homosexual conference held in late March of that year in Austin, Texas. The men involved (who had also been involved in previous disruptions) used various tactics, including the "set the chairs in a circle and let's discuss the disagreement."

The Appeal ended with:

In the judgment of GAA's delegate and of many other delegates as well, the actions . . . were well coordinated and suggested a conscious attempt deliberately to prevent the conference from doing its business. . . . Most of us are aware of examples of such divisive and destructive tactics in other recent political movements. We are aware of the damage that can be done to a movement or an organization by a handful of skilled disrupters, whether acting out of personal motivations or as a front for a less visible group or institution. . . . To avoid similar debacles in the future, GAA is attempting to compile a record of disruptions at all past gay conferences. Only by understanding what we all must deal with . . . can we prepare ourselves to deal more effectively with further attempts at disruption. We appeal to all our brothers and sisters—if you have ever been present at a conference which was disrupted, please send us information. . . . If the evidence collected suggests a pattern of disruption, the gay people have a right to know about it. If certain individuals or groups, whatever their motives, are playing games with the gay liberation movement, then the movement has a right to know about them.

GAA did not receive many reports, since protecting disrupters seems to inspire concentration of energies.

There is good money in sending "sisters" and "brothers" to jail; informing by giving names, addresses, and telephone numbers to the government, be it local or federal; getting telephones tapped; calling law enforcement agencies about planned actions (some of them initiated by agents themselves) and seeing to it that such actions are aborted and that those involved in them pay the price.

The infiltration of organizations has occurred with far more frequency than even some political activists have been prepared to believe—Watergate and recent revelations about F.B.I. and C.I.A. activities have served to reduce the skepticism of some, but many people still regard talk of infiltration as "paranoid." It is not.

Another movement problem that remains to be solved is how to channel energies and time away from repetitive and cyclical panels and workshops. Too often these conferences dissipate into circular dialogues which, in the end, evolve into still another "consciousness-raising," leaving the *cause* of oppression untouched by thought, much less action.

Misdirected energies in the lesbian movement are demonstrated in a flyer headed "The Healthy Dyke—a Panel Discussion and Workshop." This would be similar to feminists holding a work shop on how to be a "well-adjusted broad"— and one could go on: how to be a healthy "spic," "nigger," or "welfare bum." It announced a seminar on "The Well-Adjusted Dyke." When I asked women why they feel we should call ourselves by the derogatory term "dyke," I have been told that "we must reclaim our words." That the word was never "ours" but the word of the bigots who oppress us seemed to escape them. Such activity will do nothing real to achieve liberation or to combat oppression.

A similar example from the women's movement, different in that it is based on an unattainable goal: In late 1974, Ti-Grace Atkinson was invited to a Greenwich Village bookstore to autograph copies of her book *Amazon Odyssey* and to speak to the women in attendance. She was confronted by women there who told her that she had "betrayed" the young, since she did not advocate the "elimination of men, as the enemy." Since women do not have access to the kind of power to realize it, this is an unrealistic goal. It is also politically ridiculous. Ramsey Clark, good on abortion, homosexuality, and other feminist issues, would be "eliminated"; but Pat Nixon, by virtue of being a woman,

164

would remain? These women, and others who share this view, apparently don't realize that political friends are those who *act* like it, not necessarily those who by happenstance fall into prescribed areas of definition.

Another element which undermines the homosexual and the women's movements is the hostility caused by such exploitation and the complex structure of its resultant tensions. As noted, the homosexual community is composed of members of all minority and majority groups; so is the women's movement, with the exception of men. Involuted tensions within and among these and all oppressed groups are tremendous.

Although true (vertical) oppression results from the abuse of power, there is a second kind of oppression (lateral), caused by prejudice toward the alien, which results in a spiritual and mental form of oppression. This lateral oppression is exploited, however, to create chasms of ethnocentricity within and among class structures.

The structure of vertical, or power, oppression has at the top of the pyramid the white, rich males who make up the government-military-corporation complex—these men obviously hold and wield the power which keeps the rest of the structure "in place," meaning, in part, that the rest of us are rendered unoperative in the political sense. It is lateral oppression among minorities which keeps us unable to function as a unit against the downward pressure from the top.

The homosexual movement is being worked on methodically and with care. GAA had not succumbed to fragmentation to the point of dissolution; however, on October 15, 1974, the GAA Firehouse, its home for more than five years, was gutted by fire and its offices ransacked and burglarized. The New York City fire department found evidence of chemical substances on the site and assigned one investi-

165

gator to the case. Nothing has been "turned up" to date. GAA is currently meeting wherever it can and is looking for new quarters.

It seems clear that the swing of the political pendulum is to the right in a number of areas. And the homosexual does not have much time to achieve legal status. The urgency for attaining this goal is evidenced in the following article from the December 1, 1974, issue of *The New York Times:*

> WASHINGTON, Nov. 30 (UPI)—The Federal Government finances experiments to control "antisocial" human behavior with brain surgery, drugs, computers, radio transmitters implanted in the head and other means, a Senate report said today.
>
> "There is a real question whether the Government should be involved at all in programs that potentially pose substantial threats to our basic freedoms," Senator Sam J. Ervin Jr., Democrat of North Carolina, said in a preface to the 651 page report issued by his Subcommittee on Constitutional Rights. "The question becomes even more acute when these programs are conducted, as they are today, in the absence of strict controls."
>
> Behavior control technology tries to cure child molesters, homosexuals, drug abusers, alcoholics, shoplifting, hyperactive children and other "antisocial" persons through such techniques as psychosurgery—a type of brain surgery called "murder of the mind" by its critics.
>
> "The subcommittee found that the Federal Government, through a number of departments and agencies, is going ahead with behavior modification projects, including psychosurgery, without a review structure fully adequate to protect the constitutional rights of the subjects," the report said.
>
> It said the Department of Health, Education and Welfare spent the most on behavior research, but the Justice Department, Veterans Administration, Defense Depart-

ment, Labor Department and National Science Foundation were also involved.

The three-year study described an H.E.W.-funded drug-treatment program called "the seed" in the words of a South Florida high school guidance counselor:

"When they [student seedlings] return, they are 'straight,' namely quiet, well-dressed, with short hair, and not under the influence of drugs.

"However, they seem to be living in a robotlike atmosphere, they won't speak to anyone outside of their own group. Seedlings seem to have an informing system on each other and on others that is similar to Nazi Germany. They run in to use the telephone daily, to report against each other to the seed."

How blandly we homosexuals are placed in the "undesirable" column!

Considering the relative "youth" of the homosexual movement, we have made some forward strides in terms of legislation; in the following states the legislation has been changed and homosexual acts between consenting adults are not any longer considered criminal: Colorado, Connecticut, Delaware, Hawaii, Illinois, North Dakota, Ohio, and Oregon. Ordinances prohibiting discrimination on the basis of sexual orientation have been passed in the following municipalities: East Lansing, Michigan (March 1972); San Francisco, California (April 1972); Ann Arbor, Michigan (July 1972); Seattle, Washington (October 1973); Berkeley, California (November 1973); Washington, D.C. (November 1973); Detroit, Michigan (November 1973); Columbus, Ohio (January 1974); Boulder, Colorado (March 1974); Minneapolis, Minnesota (March 1974); and Alfred, New York (May 1974).

Since attitudes cannot be legislated, discrimination and

167

harassment still continue, even in these places. Others besides homosexuals who are discriminated against know that discrimination is usually disguised, and we all have heard: "Sorry, the apartment has been taken . . . the job is filled . . . sorry to let you go, but we have to cut back . . ." and so forth. However, if the homosexual can prove discrimination on the basis of sexual orientation, at least in these cities there is the promise of legal recourse.

Many people talk about coalition, but nothing on any large scale has been done about it. This is probably because each group clutches its own goals in hands which are ineffectual unless they are joined with many other hands. However, no group is willing to let go of its priorities long enough to join hands with other groups for fear of losing its grip on its own goals. But those in minorities should look to the model of the "unspoken coalition." A notable example is the meat boycott of several years ago. This was effective because everyone was doing the same thing at the same time, and nobody was saying things like: "Lesbians aren't buying either? We can't have that or people will think it's a lesbian plot;" or "Blacks aren't buying? Next they'll want to marry into our families and share our neighborhoods;" or "Welfare people are in the boycott too? We don't want people to think that *we* aren't willing to work for what we get."

The "unspoken coalition" is a rare phenomenon, but it has worked because it is the result of a basic shared goal, such as food or money, which is sought by all groups. Freedom should be considered as palpable and desirable a goal; however, individual priority and fear obscure the fact that the withholders of freedom are the same for all movements.

Only when the person on the lowest rung of the ladder is free (this person is probably a black, poor, uneducated, lesbian woman who is left-handed), only when such a person is free can we all be free.

It is to be hoped that a coalition of minorities is in the offing. A tentative step in this direction was taken in the February 1975 issue of *Ms* magazine. One hundred individual women signed a petition for freedom of sexual choice which specifically addressed itself to lesbianism as an issue, and this petition was carried in the magazine. In part it read: "In the history of women's struggle for self-determination, it has been a painful fact that almost any woman who did not choose to play a traditional or secondary role might find herself labeled a lesbian, and restricted in her efforts for fear of the effects of that label." The petition is an excellent first step. Now, I hope, organizations (with their implied numbers) in the women's and other movements will take the same step.

For years homosexuals have added their numbers (though, admittedly, often anonymously) to demonstra-strations and actions for many causes. We have worked long and hard in the feminist movement; we have demonstrated for our black sisters and brothers; we have marched with the poor and the peace demonstrators, with the American Indians, with others.

Now we expect reciprocity from other movements. Only though such a coalition against our common oppressors can we eventually form a patchwork majority from our splintered and fear-ridden minorities. Only when this is achieved will we all be able to show the power of minority numbers and purpose necessary to affect changes in our mutually shared conditions of oppression.

10

Lesbians and the Courts of Justice
Take off the Blindfold— There's a Thumb on Your Scale

> *Can there not be a government in which majorities do not virtually decide right and wrong, but conscience? in which majorities decide only those questions to which the rule of expediency is applicable? Must the citizen ever for a moment, or in the least degree, resign his conscience to the legislator? Why has every man a conscience, then? . . . It is not desirable to cultivate a respect for the law, so much as for the right. . . . Unjust laws exist: shall we be content to obey them, or shall we endeavor to amend them, and obey them until we have succeeded, or shall we transgress them at once? . . . Why is [the government] not more apt to anticipate and provide for reform? Why does it not cherish its wise minority?*
> —*Henry David Thoreau, "Civil Disobedience"*

All lesbians, all homosexuals, are born innocent of the knowledge that the natural lives which lie ahead of them have already, for centuries, been "legislated" against. The laws against our minority are not only unjust, but also un-

170

reasoning. We homosexuals "transgress them at once" in practically every single instance before we have even learned that we are "extra-legal." Then we learn that we are not only "extra-legal," but "extra-moral" as well, since the statutes against us declare that homosexuals are "sexual deviates." "Sexual deviates" are in turn legally defined as "of bad moral character."

We learn too, if we probe the laws and their meaning, of the many areas in which we are "legally" denied our civil rights. For example, in all but eight states,* *known* homosexuals are denied state licenses, or these licenses can be revoked if anyone holding one is found to be homosexual. Known homosexuals are also ineligible for bonding.

The following are some of the licensed professions which we cannot *legally* pursue in forty-two of the United States**:

accountant	coast guard officer
aircraft mechanic	co-pilot
architect	cosmetologist
attorney	dental hygienist
audiologist	dentist
barber	electrician
bar owner	electric-sign service-
beautician	person
broadcast transmitter	electronics technician
(operator and adjuster)	(radio and television)
bus driver	engineer—all fields
cabaret owner	entertainer requiring
certain civil service	a cabaret license
employees	fireman
chauffeur	flight engineer
chiropractor	independent psychologist
clergy—all religions	insurance agent

* Exceptions: Connecticut, Illinois, Ohio, Colorado, Delaware, Hawaii, North Dakota, and Oregon.
** Source: United States Department of Labor. *Occupational Outlook Handbook,* 1970–1971, ed. Bureau of Labor Statistics.

lawyer
licensed merchant
  marine officer
licensed practical nurse
liquor store owner
maintenance electrician
optical mechanic
optician
optometrist
pharmacist
physician—all fields
pilot
pipe fitter
plumber
podiatrist
police officer

radiotelephone operator
real estate broker
real estate salesperson
registered nurse
school counselor
securities salesperson
state trooper
taxicab driver
teacher—all fields
  and grade levels
television and radio
  repairperson
truck and bus mechanic
truck driver
veterinarian

The field of education represents a double indemnity of discrimination. On the one hand, sex education classes in school, if they include information on homosexuality at all, present negative and confused attitudes about it to the young. On the other hand, homosexuals are, later in life, barred from the teaching profession on the premise that they are of bad moral character and child molesters. This is ironical since it is the male teacher who most often seduces young female students. In her statement at the 1971 New York hearings on victimless crimes, Ellen Povill said, in part:

> One of the reasons that homosexuals are not permitted to teach is the myth in our culture that homosexuals are child molesters. Child molesters are pederasts, not homosexuals. This myth is one of the untruths that should be cleared up via education at an adult level. . . . Because of our puritan-sexist society, practically all children grow to adulthood in a mist of confusion about sexuality. The child has no way of dealing cor-

172

rectly with her feelings. . . . If sex education classes explained homosexuality as one natural way of life, homosexual children would understand what is going on inside of them. Without such classes these children are placed in a degrading, outcast position.

I would like to give one example of children's ignorance about homosexuality. Two weeks ago I was walking along Central Park West holding hands with another woman. Suddenly a large piece of concrete slammed into the building less than a foot behind us. The concrete shattered at our feet. We looked around and found it had been thrown at us from across the street by a group of seven teenage girls. When they saw we had spotted them a barrage of smaller rocks were thrown at us. These girls knew so little about lesbianism, and evidently had their personal fears about us, that they hollered the word "fags" several times. It seems "lesbian" is not even in their vocabulary. I doubt this would have happened had they received proper sex education.

The New York Times of November 12, 1972, carried this news story:

BALTIMORE, Nov. 11—A homosexual has filed a suit in Federal District Court here accusing a Maryland school board of unconstitutionally keeping him from his classroom.

Joseph Acanfora 3d said that he had filed the suit against the Montgomery County Board of Education because the board had transferred him to a non-teaching post and had given him no indication if or when it would permit him to teach again.

He was transferred in September from his job as an eighth-grade teacher of earth sciences at Parkland Junior High School, Rockville, soon after a Pennsylvania dispute about his homosexuality was publicized here. His new post is in the school district's department of curriculum.

As a senior at Pennsylvania State University last February, Mr. Acanfora brought suit against the university seeking equal rights for homosexuals, which he contended the university denied.

When his suit became public, he was promptly dismissed as a student teacher. Later, he was reinstated by a court.

After he was graduated in June, however, the University Teachers Certification Council deadlocked, 3 to 3, on whether he could meet provisions of Pennsylvania law requiring teachers to be "of good moral character."

The State Secretary of Education, forced to act without a council recommendation, approved Mr. Acanfora's teaching credentials on Sept. 22.

Mr. Acanfora, who is a resident of Brick Township, N. J., and rents an apartment in Washington during the school year, said that he did not tell anyone he was a homosexual when he applied for his job. He asserts that this information is not pertinent.

The National Education Association is financing his suit.

The "60 Minutes" CBS television program of February 25, 1973, gave a report on Mr. Acanfora's ongoing court battle. As part of the program, a reporter interviewed people in the community regarding their attitudes. One woman said that she thought Mr. Acanfora was a very good and dedicated teacher and she didn't see any reason for removing him from his teaching position. However, a local clergyman was shown talking to a community group, stressing that it must not allow a "pervert" to move among its children and corrupt morals. No matter how good a teacher he might be, Mr. Acanfora will be forced to seek another profession which doesn't require a Pennsylvania state license. The court decision went against him.

There are other areas in which homosexuals are denied their civil rights as a result of their extra-legal status. The

174

commitment a homosexual couple may feel for each other is ineligible for legal sanction. (The homosexual marriage ceremonies performed in the few gay churches in the country are not legal. They are performed by clergymen [invited out of their religious orders] because of their avowed homosexuality; perhaps the best known is the Reverend Troy Perry, who formed one of the earliest gay churches, in New York City. These "marriages" may bring spiritual sustenance to those involved but they are not contractual.) Thus the homosexual couple are not permitted the benefits of maintaining a joint household such as filing joint income tax returns, securing loans, leases, and titles to property, acquiring mortgages and insurance ratings on the basis of their status as a couple.

Although the marriage contract is in itself oppressive and a carry-over from heterosexual society, it is an inequity that homosexuals (as well as unmarried heterosexual couples) cannot receive the same benefits, especially as our taxes are used in so many ways against us.

On the subjecet of marriage and homosexuality, the following appeared on January 7, 1973, in *The New York Times:*

> MINNEAPOLIS, Minn.—Jack Baker, an outspoken leader of the Gay Liberation Movement, has been ruled eligible for the Minnesota bar examination by examiners who found that he did not fraudulently obtain the license with which he entered into a homosexual marriage.
>
> Mr. Baker was graduated from the University of Minnesota Law School in December, while serving his second term as student president.
>
> After he applied for the bar examination the State Board of Law Examiners invited him to a hearing to answer questions about his 1971 application for a marriage license in Mankato, Minn.

At issue was a state law that requires candidates for the bar and for other professions, to be of "good moral character."

A question had been raised, not about Mr. Baker's avowed homosexuality, but about his responses in applying for the marriage license.

In early 1970, Mr. Baker and James Michael McConnell, both now 30 years old, applied for a license in Minneapolis but were refused. Supported by the Minnesota civil liberties union, they carried an appeal to the United States Supreme Court, which dismissed the case last October "for want of a substantial Federal question."

During the appeal period, Mr. Baker and Mr. McConnell pursued other avenues toward union. On Aug. 3, 1972, Mr. McConnell legally adopted Mr. Baker in Minneapolis, with the goal of securing tax and inheritance advantages.

At that time, Mr. Baker legally assumed the name Pat Lynn McConnell, while continuing to use the name Baker in his daily affairs. Shortly after the adoption, Mr. Baker signed his new name to a marriage license application in Mankato, a college city 80 miles southwest of Minneapolis. On Aug. 16, 1971, Blue Earth County issued the license, and, on Sept. 3, Mr. Baker and Mr. McConnell were married in a private ceremony in Minneapolis by the Rev. Roger Lynn of the United Methodist Church.

Shortly after the ceremony John Corbey, the Blue Earth County attorney, said that the license was defective and the marriage null and void because the address listed on the application "was not that of the bride." Minnesota law required that marriage licenses be issued in the county of the bride's residence, and the address listed by Mr. Baker was that of a vacationing professor.

Subsequently, the Hennepin County grand jury studied the legality of the marriage but found the question not worth pursuing. Thus the marriage remained in effect.

After the bar examiners studied the same issue last month, William J. Lloyd, the director of bar admissions in Minnesota, wrote to Mr. Baker, saying that the board "will make no objection to your application, which will be processed in due course."

Mr. Baker plans to take the bar examination in February. But, he said, "as far as I'm concerned, the last hurdle hasn't been met." If he passes the bar, he still must be sworn in by the Minnesota Supreme Court.

Mr. Baker lost his case in court. He was not sworn in.

The restrictive marital institution, as created and enforced by the church, produces many victims, specifically anyone who operates outside that institution. Perhaps the most blatant victim of church-state laws is the child of unwed parents.* The church places the "bastard" stigma on the child, which she or he carries for the rest of life, as though the child, rather than the parents, had "transgressed the law."

The way the courts and laws act against homosexuals as opposed to other minority members is doubly tainted, since the homosexual label automatically carries with it the "immorality" label. The repeated defeats of the gay rights bill in New York City, for instance, tends to reinforce in many minds the "validity" of the laws against us. The thought is that if the legislation can't pass after all these tries, the "immorality" is evident.

Another aspect of this problem is how same-sex assaults or murders are always labeled "homosexual" or "homo," inferring that homosexuality, rather than criminality, is at fault. Rape-killings, child assaults, and other attacks on fe-

---

* I know the phrase always used is "unwed mother," as though the mother were the only unwed person involved in the situation; more realistically, I use "unwed parents."

177

males by males are not called "heterosexual crimes," which would indeed reflect adversely on heterosexuality. This is important inasmuch as prejudicial labeling of crimes as "homosexual" helps tip the balance of justice against homosexuals not only in the courts but in the minds of the general public, from which future juries will be chosen.

The "bad moral character" charge against us is almost always misused against homosexual mothers or fathers who seek divorce. Lesbians involved in divorce and custody cases face a nightmare. They must remain vigilantly closeted lest it becomes known that they are homosexual. A lesbian is automatically regarded as an "unfit mother" in the eyes of the law, and her child or children can be taken from her. It is tragically ironic that in many instances of severe child abuse by heterosexual mothers, the courts return the child to the "natural mother"; apparently such mothers are considered by the courts to be more fit than a loving lesbian mother. There have been many instances of lawyers giving up hope of any child custody settlement in the mother's favor if it became known that the mother was lesbian. The minute the word homosexuality is uttered, many lawyers simply throw up their hands.

The American Civil Liberties Union acknowledges the severe problems facing such women. For those who think that homosexuals have recourse through the courts, consider these points:

A lesbian mother in a custody battle does not have to prove that she is a fit mother; instead, she must *disprove* that she is an unfit mother of bad moral character. And, according to A.C.L.U., she is required to provide "extreme amounts of evidence, including a psychiatrist who will testify that she is not 'crazy.' " She must also be able to produce "a ridiculous number of character witnesses."

Mr. Baker lost his civil liberties case in court, not because he was "an avowed homosexual," but rather because of what the court called, in lay language, "his bizarre *manifestation* of his homosexuality." In other words, because he was openly living within his needs of a contractual marriage. He was "too honest."

In Mr. Acanfora's case, the Supreme Court refused to overturn the lower-court decision because prior to application for his teaching job he had been openly active in the homosexual movement; however, on the application form under the designation for "Other Activities" (where most people write "tennis," or "chess," or "playing in a chamber music group") Mr. Acanfora did not list his activities in the gay movement. He was "not honest enough." Catch 22.

We must remove the thumb from the scale of justice. For me and my people it has been there for centuries. It is there for all minorities. Only we, the minorities, can remove it, because the system will not cure itself. The system considers itself to be in the best of health. And it is—it is doing well.

We, you and I, are not.

If the archaic anti-homosexual laws on the books are valid, they should be enforced whenever a person's homosexuality becomes known. If these are valid laws, they should not be used only to threaten those who operate politically. If these are valid laws, they should not be used only to harass, oppress, and fragment organizations with goals of equal treatment, equal rights, and equal dignity under the law.

If they are not valid laws, they should be removed from the books, because laws which cannot be or are not enforced equally are corrupt laws, for they can be misused as a tool of oppression.

With all of this in mind, I feel obligated to make a statement. I have checked with lawyers and I make my statement in full knowledge of its possible consequences. If I were a scoff-law and had accumulated five hundred traffic violation tickets, if I were a thief and had burgled banks or stores or homes and planned to continue in these activities, I could in the same way invoke the validity of the laws against my actions and the enforcement of such laws:

I, as a "sexual deviate of bad moral character," have "committed crimes against Nature" in the past. I am currently "committing" such acts, and I plan to "commit" such acts in the future.

On the day this book is published I will hold a press conference. A news release and invitation to attend will be sent to media representatives and to my local police precinct. If no police attend, or if a representative is there but does not make an arrest, a knowledgeable person of political integrity who will be in attendance will, in an act of friendship and understanding, make a civil arrest and take me to the police precinct. The event and its consequences will be recorded and reported by the media.

If the laws against homosexuality are valid laws and not disguises for other things, then I expect police and legal action against me. If no such action is taken against me, we can assume that the laws are not valid.

If the latter should be the case, what then are such laws doing on the books?

Who is responsible for allowing these laws to stand? Does the responsibility lie with you . . . with me . . . with us?